"This master negotiator shares his best practices and proven techniques that will change the way you do business. Learn how to perfect the art of negotiation through his insightful wisdom. A must-read for the serious business professional!"

—Nido Qubein, president of High Point University
and chairman of Great Harvest Bread Company

"For neophytes and experts alike, this masterful little book will immediately increase your negotiating effectiveness and dramatically improve your bottom line."

—Daniel Burrus, author of *Technotrends*

"Jim Hennig has laid out a flight plan that avoids turbulence in negotiation, which we all encounter daily. Planning your strategy in advance is key to maintaining relationships and successful outcomes. Everyone can learn from what Jim shares from his vast experience. Put this on your must-read list."

—Howard Putnam, former CEO of Southwest Airlines
and author of *The Winds of Turbulence*

"*Negotiating to Win* brings an exciting new set of tools to the table. Jim Hennig communicates like no one else on negotiation."

—Rita Davenport, president of Arbonne International

"A surefire way to take your negotiating skills to the next level. *Negotiating to Win* summarizes Jim Hennig's two decades of training expertise with tens of thousands of people from all walks of life. It's a quick read, but over three hundred powerful real-life examples make it easy to apply. You'll see immediate bottom line results."

—Tom Hopkins, author of *How to Master the Art of Selling*

"Informative! Entertaining! Practical! Jim's unique negotiating philosophy, his masterful teaching skills, and hundreds of real-life examples will make an immediate improvement in your negotiating effectiveness."

—Bob Danzig, former CEO of Hearst Newspapers, author,
and member of the Speakers' Hall of Fame

continued . . .

P9-CCE-520

"Just do it! Read this book, follow its advice, and you'll be able to 'do it' in an exemplary way. This highly readable and practical book gives you dozens of real-world examples that have been field-tested and ready to go! And when you practice and use the 'partnering principles,' you're assured of being just that much better in all of your negotiation activities. Dr. Hennig's easy-to-follow tips and techniques will make you a real winner!"

—Edward E. Scannell, CMP, CSP, former president of the American Society for Training and Development, Meeting Professionals International, and the National Speakers Association, and coauthor of the Games Trainers Play series

"The more I travel around the world, speaking to corporations and meeting all kinds of people, the more I realize one common, simple truth: building positive relationships is the key to success. Jim's philosophy of building relationships by finding and meeting the real needs of both parties through the use of questions, effective listening, honesty, integrity, sincere caring, and partnerships is so brilliantly taught throughout this book. This is a must-read for anyone wanting to evolve from mediocrity to greatness, in every area of their life!"

—Les Brown, motivational speaker and bestselling author

"This is the best book on effective negotiating you will ever read! It is fast-moving, practical, and loaded with simple strategies you can use to get the best deal every time."

—Brian Tracy, author of The Way to Wealth

"After more than forty years as a salesman, employer, author, and speaker, I thought I knew almost everything there was to know about negotiating. Jim Hennig proves that you can teach an old dog new tricks!"

—Harvey Mackay, #1 New York Times bestselling author of Swim with the Sharks

HOW TO SAY IT®

Negotiating to Win

*Key Words, Phrases, and
Strategies to Close the Deal and
Build Lasting Relationships*

Jim Hennig, PhD

PRENTICE HALL PRESS

PRENTICE HALL PRESS
Published by the Penguin Group
Penguin Group (USA) Inc.
375 Hudson Street, New York, New York 10014, USA
Penguin Group (Canada), 90 Eglinton Avenue East, Suite 700, Toronto,
Ontario M4P 2Y3, Canada (a division of Pearson Penguin Canada Inc.) •
Penguin Books Ltd., 80 Strand, London WC2R 0RL, England • Penguin Group
Ireland, 25 St. Stephen's Green, Dublin 2, Ireland (a division of Penguin Books
Ltd.) • Penguin Group (Australia), 250 Camberwell Road, Camberwell, Victoria
3124, Australia (a division of Pearson Australia Group Pty. Ltd.) • Penguin Books
India Pvt. Ltd., 11 Community Centre, Panchsheel Park, New Delhi—110 017,
India • Penguin Group (NZ), 67 Apollo Drive, Rosedale, North Shore 0632, New
Zealand (a division of Pearson New Zealand Ltd.) • Penguin Books (South Africa)
(Pty.) Ltd., 24 Sturdee Avenue, Rosebank, Johannesburg 2196, South Africa

Penguin Books Ltd., Registered Offices: 80 Strand, London WC2R 0RL,
England

First edition: August 2008

Library of Congress Cataloging-in-Publication Data

Hennig, Jim.
How to say it negotiating to win : key words, phrases, and strategies to close
the deal and build lasting relationship / Jim Hennig.
p. cm.
ISBN-13: 978-0-7352-0428-7
1. Negotiation in business. 2. Negotiation. 3. Business networks. I. Title.
HD58.6.H464 2008
658.4'052—dc22   2008015092

PRINTED IN THE UNITED STATES OF AMERICA

10 9 8 7 6 5 4 3 2 1

To my dear family,
who taught me as I negotiated with them,
the most important principle of life:
Relationships are what matters most.

To the love of my life, and my best friend, Coreen;

To my ideal parents, Margaret and Fred,
whom I miss dearly;

To my angel sister, Julie, and John, and their
wonderful family;

To my loving, caring children and stepchildren, Dawn,
Troy, Ryan, Tara, Robert, Ashley, Dan, Phil, Rob, and
Kellen.

Acknowledgments

To Coreen, who read and reread, and listened to me patiently for years.

To Mary Gainey, whose unfailing dedication kept the business afloat and the office organized while I wrote.

To my agent, Barry Neville, who started the whole process and whose expertise secured the contract for this work.

To my editor, Maria Gagliano, who spent untold hours in turning my very rough draft into a polished manuscript, despite my stubbornness.

To the doctors and staff at Advanced Cardiac Specialist, who tenderly and skillfully nursed my ailing heart through fifteen angioplasties and two heart attacks.

To the doctors and staff at Mayo Clinic Hospital/Scottsdale, whose caring skill and unsurpassed expertise replaced my dying heart with a healthy one, which made this book and my life now possible. It is truly great to be alive.

To the special heart donor and his valiant family, to whom I am eternally indebted.

To my hundreds of corporate clients, and tens of thousands of individuals who have cooperated with me in gathering examples, testing principles, proving guidelines, validating concepts, developing strategies and tactics, and, most important, confirming the effectiveness of the techniques taught in my programs and in this book.

Contents

Introduction

Negotiating to Win is the class they never taught you in high school or college (but should have). Negotiation is one of the most important skills anyone can learn. It can be your ticket to greater success, happiness, and prosperity.

What is negotiating, anyway? I define it this way: *Negotiation is any situation in which two or more parties interact, with at least one party seeking to gain from the interaction.* Ask successful people what skill is most important to their success and they'll almost always tell you, "Negotiation."

The art of *putting together the deal* is the most important skill you can learn.

Whether you are a business executive, parent, teacher, salesperson, entrepreneur, nurse, CPA, lawyer, politician, or whatever . . . we all negotiate many times each day. It may be:

- Buying or selling your home or automobile
- Asking for a raise and negotiating benefits at work
- Deciding with your spouse where to go on vacation
- Negotiating that big deal with your most important client

- Persuading your five-year-old to eat her vegetables
- Doing *anything at all* with your teenager

Some of these negotiations will save or make you hundreds and sometimes hundreds of thousands of dollars. Others build or destroy relationships that are priceless. Sometimes the latter outcomes are more important than the former. Regardless, much is at stake.

Nevertheless, I often hear my clients say, "I hate to negotiate. I don't want to be adversarial. I don't want to get in someone's face. If negotiation means I have to be willing to do that, forget it! I would rather just pay whatever they ask! I read those books many years ago and that was the message—right?" Wrong! It might have worked ten years ago, but times have changed. Most people are much more sophisticated now. They have more negotiating knowledge and experience.

How did you feel the last time someone used strong-arm tactics and intimidation to jam a deal down your throat? No one likes it. These tactics get short-term results at best. In the end, the price may be too high to pay. What if you could get what you want without being a bad guy? You can. That's what this book is all about.

My basic philosophy of negotiating is this:

Build relationships by finding and meeting the real needs of both you and the other party through the use of questions, effective listening, honesty, integrity, sincere caring, and building partnerships.

Sound altruistic? It is! But when you *can* be altruistic, and almost always get more out of the negotiation than you would by using conventional adversarial techniques, why not do it? The reason this philosophy of negotiation works is simple. *When people like you, they want to work with you.* They are likely to concede more often. They become more sensitive to your needs, and more likely to try to meet them.

When people like you, they want to work with you!

You may negotiate with some who feel they couldn't care less about the other party. They just want the best deal they can get regardless of what it takes to get it. There are two ways of dealing with this type of negotiator:

- Walk away. It's fun to do if you have alternatives.
- Know all the basic negotiating concepts. When you know what the other party is doing, their strategies, tactics, techniques, and tricks become much less effective.

This book will arm you with everything you need to know about negotiating so you can take this latter approach whenever necessary.

Chapters 1 and 2 contain the techniques (asking and listening, respectively) to learn *the other party's real needs*. Each party in a negotiation has two types of needs:

- Their needs relating to the negotiation at hand
- Their needs relating to their unique personality

style (how they prefer to negotiate, how they like to be treated, etc.)

This is why every negotiation is different. Either the "negotiation needs" or the "personal needs"—or both—change. In short, the whole ball game changes. Negotiation is not only a *skill* based on principles (which can and will be taught in this book), but it's also an *art* (which can only be learned through the experience of applying these principles).

One fact has become clear after years of observation. *Good* negotiators understand the importance of, and quickly identify, the other party's *negotiation needs*. *Great* negotiators understand the importance of, and quickly identify, the other party's *personal needs*, in addition to their negotiation needs.

The first two chapters constitute the most important information in the entire book because they teach the two skills essential for finding needs. Pay particular attention to chapter 1, "The Power of Questions." It's not that asking is more important than listening. They are equally important. The difference is this: *asking is a skill that can be taught; listening is an art motivated by the heart.* In other words, the process of learning to ask questions requires knowing what to ask and how to ask it. The art of effective listening, although there are some techniques that can be taught, depends more on the listener's motivation to listen than on one's acquired skills to improve listening.

Chapter 3, "Power Factors," enables you to assess your own power and the power of the other party, and then shows you how to maximize your own power.

When you master these three negotiating cornerstones (questions, listening, and power), you lay a strong foundation for the additional skills taught in the remaining chapters of the book, including:

- Getting and Giving Concessions
- Negotiating from a Weak Position
- Handling Difficult Negotiators
- Alternatives at an Impasse
- Body Language
- Telephone Techniques
- Team Negotiating
- Strategies and Tactics
- Avoiding Common Errors

This book is designed to be used as a quick reference guide as well as an informative, straight-through read. I hope you will take the time to read it from cover to cover, but you may find it even more valuable as a reference guide to consult before, during, and after a negotiation. Continuing to review the strategies, tactics, techniques, and guidelines in this book, particularly in close proximity to your actual negotiations, will firmly implant them as habits and not just abstract ideas or philosophical concepts. For this reason, some similar concepts may be shared in more than one chapter, with cross-references supplied in the text.

PARTNERING PRINCIPLES

A number of years ago I was fascinated by certain people's ability to build relationships—to partner with others to accomplish what was important to both of them. Some people had it . . . some people didn't. But what was "it"? What was that special ingredient that made you want to be around them . . . that made you want to do business with them . . . that made you feel like their friend? I had to know! I had to find out.

So I began an extensive study of people who were really good at partnering, at relationship building. It took a long time to begin to see patterns, but slowly and surely, they began to take shape. One thing, more than anything else, seemed to rise to the surface as the essence of relationship building and the essence of partnering. It's simple:

People do business with people they like.

People like to do business with people who really care about them! Now this may not come as a shock to most of you. "As a matter of fact," you might say, "I've known that for years. It's obvious."

What is not so obvious is what they are doing that makes the other parties know they *really care*. I decided that if I could determine what those principles or characteristics were, then I'd really have something.

So I continued to observe. Again, certain principles slowly began to emerge. The more I studied great partners, and what caused their partnerships to be so successful—whether it be family, social, or business partnerships—the more my thinking crystallized. Over many years, principles evolved that describe *how* people communicate with other people they really care for. Below are the partnering principles that great negotiators seem to have mastered.

1. Act as if the Relationship Will Last Forever

Let's be practical. Will it last forever? No, except perhaps with your spouse or family, or maybe a best friend. So 95 to 99 percent of the time the relationship won't last forever. And for many of your negotiations it will be a one-shot deal—you'll never see them again. But here is the key: when you act as if the relationship will last forever—and really care about the other party—something happens that's hard to explain (without getting into karma!).

For example, when I sold my aircraft and my home in preparation for our move to Arizona, it was important for me to find just the right person for these two items. I had enjoyed them so much and wanted them to go to someone who would get the same satisfaction out of them that I did. I treated the potential buyer in each case as if the relationship would last forever. It didn't—it was about a week in one case and about a month in the other. But when the details got sticky on both deals near the end, the sales would not have gone through had it not been for the relationship we had built.

This principle—act as if the relationship will last forever—is the cornerstone of the partnering principles and thus one of the most important concepts in the entire book. The remaining seven principles provide additional examples of how to do this. You will also find this concept woven through much of the rest of the book.

2. Understand Needs and Wants—the Other Party's and Your Own

> *Always get to know the other party.*
> *Never negotiate with a stranger.*
> —Somers White

Work as hard to satisfy the other party's needs and wants as you do your own!

Example: When I was first developing these partnering principles, I began experimenting with them in my own business. I was talking with my attorney, who had a copy of the principles, about copyright and trademark protection. He explained that his firm had a standard package to accomplish this for a flat fee of just under $1,000.

Looking to gain some alternative power, I asked him, "Is there any other way to do it?"

"Sure, you could file it yourself, Jim. The fee is about $250, which, of course, is included in our price."

"David, do you believe these partnering principles are a good way to do business?"

"Yes, sounds like a great concept."

"Will you apply them with me in this transaction?"

After a pause, he said, "Yes."

"David, I trust you, and I'm going to follow your advice whatever it is, because I know you will act in both of our best interests. Here's my question: should I file it myself or take your package deal for a grand?"

There was another pause, this one a little longer. Then, very excitedly, he said, "Jim, I've got it. I'll fax you the form. You or your staff can fill it out the best you can. Fax it back to me and I'll tweak it at my hourly rate. I'll bet you'll save $500!"

"David, you're a great attorney—I'll take your advice!"

Now, obviously, it was a win for me—I easily saved $500. But what about David? You might say, "Well, he lost $500." Actually, David accomplished two things:

- He got my business and my loyalty.
- I've already referred him to many others who have paid him fees many times the $500 he may have "lost" on my deal.

In short, David worked as hard to meet my needs as he did his own; what comes around goes around.

3. Adopt a "They," Not "You," Orientation

The Golden Rule states: "Do unto others as *you* would have them do unto *you*." Notice that the emphasis is on *you*.

The Platinum Rule (as described by Tony Alessandra in his book of the same name) changes the thought slightly: "Do unto others as *they* would have you do unto *them*."

Notice that the emphasis is on *them*. In other words, treat other people the way *they* want to be treated, not the way *you* want to be treated. Let's face it—people are different. Treat them differently. Specifically, treat them the way they want to be treated.

Example: You are on the telephone with someone who is speaking very, very slowly. You want to be effective with this individual, but they are driving you nuts because they talk so very slowly. The Golden Rule or the Platinum Rule? If you want to be effective, you choose the Platinum Rule. You slow down. They begin to feel comfortable. You've treated them the way they want to be treated. They are happy, comfortable, and much more likely to help you get what you want.

4. Recognize Feelings as Facts

Example: Sometimes my wife feels upset and there is no good reason for her to feel that way. If I could only help her to see why she shouldn't feel that way, everything would be fine. How am I doing, spouses? Not very well at all, am I?

When the other party feels hurt, offended, taken advantage of, unappreciated, or any other positive or negative emotion, it should be considered as *fact*. That *is* the way they feel. Initially, it's not important whether they "should" or "should not" feel that way.

In every negotiation, first understand exactly how the other party feels.

Ask, "How do you feel about . . . [name the issue]?" Then, if appropriate, ask, "Can you help me understand better?" Ask as many additional questions as necessary to be sure you understand how they feel and why they feel that way.

Then you might continue with, "Now, let me make sure . . . what I think I hear you saying is that you feel . . . [restate their response in your own words]. Is that correct?" Acknowledge their feelings as facts. Then decide the appropriate course of action.

While teaching at Purdue University, I knew a wonderful professor by the name of Charles Riker. He emphasized "FFTT"—Feelings First, Then Think!—in every communication training that he facilitated. He emphasized that you can't *think clearly* until you understand how you are *feeling*. First, know what you (and the other party) are feeling. Then you can begin to tackle the difficult challenges of the negotiation.

"Feelings first, then think!"
—Dr. Charles Riker

My wife will frequently say, "Jim, thanks for listening. That helped me crystallize my feelings. Now I know what to do." I didn't need to help her solve whatever was on her mind; I just need to listen.

5. Take No Personal Offense

Great negotiators understand the danger of taking personal offense. They have conditioned themselves never to allow that to happen—even if the offense is intentional! Taking offense only escalates negative emotions and creates obstacles in the negotiation itself.

Example: Years ago one of my sons decided he wanted to become an airline pilot. The most practical way to get the hours and the advanced ratings he required was to purchase a small, training aircraft. After surveying what was available, we found one that looked like the perfect aircraft for us. After reviewing pictures and specifications and negotiating a price, we made a tentative deal by phone. It would be contingent upon inspection of the aircraft when we arrived at the small Idaho airport where it was kept.

After a brief inspection, I mentioned to the owner that the exterior paint looked much worse than the pictures had portrayed and I wanted to make a few calls before we made a final decision.

We did buy the aircraft, and after completing the paperwork, while we were preparing to depart, the former owner told me, "I had to catch myself after your comment about the paint. I taught myself long ago that personal offense plays no constructive part in a negotiation. I'm glad I caught myself. We might not have put the deal together." I then took the opportunity to apologize to him for not being more sensitive to his feelings. It was certainly not my intent to offend or imply any deception on his part.

How many negotiations stall and never reach a successful conclusion because one or both of the parties take personal offense? Think of it this way—no one can offend you without your permission. All they can do is say things or take actions that might facilitate your taking offense. Only *you* can take it. *Don't.* You'll have an infinitely greater chance of reaching an acceptable conclusion.

No one can offend you without your permission!

---

6. Use Your Power to Build Relationships

Negotiators often unwisely use the power they have for immediate gain. Frequently, your power can be more effectively used to build long-term relationships.

Example: An acquaintance invited me to coauthor a major project. He said he had already invested $60,000 in research. After thoroughly investigating his background and the project, I decided to do it. Our agreement enabled him to recoup the $60,000 out of the first proceeds. About a month after signing the agreement, he came to me and said that his accountant had just discovered, and informed him, that the research cost was actually only $40,000. "We've got to change the contract, Jim," he said to me. Wow! Talk about honesty! Talk about using power to cement relationships! You can guess where my trust level stood with this newly acquired partner.

Another example: A client company asked me to develop an audio program specifically designed to cover real estate negotiations. I would do all the writing and be the voice for the recording. The client would cover all production costs. I would hold the copyright and have my contact information on the product. They would pay me a royalty each time they used the program with their people. I, in turn, would be able to purchase the program at cost for resale to my other clients and on my website. This is a perfect example of how they used their power to create an ideal situation for both of us.

7. Have Honest, Open Communications

Just how important is honesty in a negotiation? I'll admit that in some negotiations lying will help forward your cause. Is it worth it? Only you can answer that question. Perhaps it can best be answered with this question: how long does it take to get someone's trust back once you've lost it through dishonesty? Most likely, you will never get it back! As Mark Twain once said, "If you tell the truth, you don't have to remember anything."

Example: I was selling my aircraft to an eager buyer who had responded to my ad. I said, "Do you want to know the good things or the bad things about my aircraft first?"

"The bad things," was his obvious response.

"In heavy rain and instrument flight conditions, the #1 communication radio will sometimes develop static, making it hard to hear the controller. I've had it in the shop twice but they have been unable to isolate the problem. I did find, however, that the problem could easily be solved by switching to the #2 communication radio. After a few minutes, you can switch back to #1 and you'll not have another problem with it."

I proceeded to point out two other minor problems. I was concerned that these three problems might jeopardize my chance for a sale. After that, he wanted to know the good things about the aircraft, of which there were many. After purchasing the aircraft that day, he said, "Jim, I knew I could trust you (and the aircraft) once you told me of the radio problem. I obviously would not have found that out in our test flight because we wouldn't be test flying in instrument conditions. I had pretty much made up my mind to buy the aircraft right then."

I believe honesty is the best policy—even if it hurts the negotiation. You'd be surprised how often the reverse is true. Mark Twain also said, "Honesty is the best policy—when there is money in it."

The second part of this important partnering principle

is *open communication*. Here's what I found: people who are good at building thriving partnerships seem to share more information that is personal (or what might be considered "confidential" information). Don't misunderstand me—obviously, there is some information that (in almost all situations) should remain confidential. However, if you are willing to share some information that the other party considers as your confidential information, they are more likely to share also. It makes sense—the more two parties know about each other's situation, the more likely they are to put together a mutually satisfying deal.

8. Determine Ahead of Time How to Resolve Differences

The time to resolve differences is *before* they happen . . . before negative emotions develop . . . before tempers flare . . . before feelings are hurt. What is easy to discuss beforehand is very difficult to discuss when you're in the middle of a heated disagreement.

In a simple partnership, you might say something like this: "Kathy, our partnership is really important to me and I know it is to you also. I'd hate to have a disagreement get in the way of our friendship or our business relationship. Let's agree to this: if we ever disagree and can't seem to resolve the difference, let's allow Tricia to decide what would be a fair resolution of the problem. I know you trust Tricia to be fair and I do also. I'll agree to abide by her decision, how about you?"

In a more formal situation, you may want to agree to using the American Arbitration Association guidelines (www.adr.org) before either party takes formal legal action. George Herbert penned this insightful thought in 1640: "A lean compromise is better than a fat lawsuit."

These eight partnering principles create the strong foundation underlying the information (techniques, strategies, guidelines, tactics, philosophies) in the twelve chapters that follow. Think of each chapter as a room in your house. Each performs a different function. Some negotiators are strong in certain areas (rooms). However, it is important to be a well-balanced negotiator, not just one who is strong in a couple of areas. How effective and desirable would a home be without a kitchen? How effective would a negotiator be if she lacked the ability to listen . . . to ask questions . . . to recover from a weak position . . . or to overcome a critical impasse in a negotiation?

As you approach each chapter, evaluate your ability and skill in that area. Pay particular attention to those areas in which you feel less than adequate. Like the house without a kitchen, you will find yourself only as strong as your weakest link. By the time you reach the conclusion, you'll feel a new sense of confidence and will look forward to your next negotiation.

PART 1

Before the Negotiation Begins

Things you need to be aware of before you start

1
The Power of Questions

Judge a man by his questions
rather than by his answers.
—Voltaire

There's a very good reason why I'm starting this book with a discussion of questions. It goes back to my basic philosophy of negotiating: *build relationships by finding and meeting real needs.* How do you find needs? Ask questions. What percentage of your negotiating time do you spend asking questions and then listening to the answers? You're likely to spend more time talking than asking or listening. Virtually anyone can increase their negotiating effectiveness by asking more effective questions. This is because the better you know the other party's needs, the more likely you'll be to meet those needs and therefore have more power.

FUNCTIONS OF QUESTIONS

Why does a good negotiator ask questions? What are the functions of questions in the negotiation process?

1. To Get Someone's Attention

Some questions speak to what people want but are having a problem getting. Starting with "If . . ." or "Suppose that . . ." is a good way to do this.

• *"Suppose that we lost electric power for an extended time because of a natural disaster? How would you and your family do?"* (To encourage someone to buy a generator.)

• *"If I could show you a way you can save money on refinancing your home, would you be interested?"*

• *"Children, if I could show you a way we could all go to Disneyland, would you be interested?"* (Is there any question that you now have the kids' undivided attention?)

• *"How do you feel about that?"* Normally used to get information, this question could get the attention of someone who tends to base their decisions on their *feelings*. It makes sense to them and therefore gets their attention if they think you are interested.

• *"What do you think about that?"* Use this with people who you know tend to base their decisions on logic. It makes sense to them. Note that these last two questions are essentially the same. The first is more comfortable to a person who makes decisions primarily based on their feelings. The second is more comfortable to the person who makes decisions primarily based on logic or thinking. Thus we are applying the Platinum Rule—treating people the way *they*, not you or someone else, want to be treated (see page 9).

2. To Get Information

This is obviously the most common function of a question. Who? What? Why? Where? When? How? Knowledge is power in a negotiation, particularly knowledge of the other party and their needs. Ask the right question, in the right way, at the right time, and then listen carefully to the answer. Here are some examples of good questions that get valuable information:

• *"What else can you tell me?"* Just assuming there is more information to be shared normally draws out valuable information.

• *"Is the offer [proposal, position] clear?"* Make this a standard question after making an offer. Be sure the other party's perception of the offer is what you intended the offer to be. The other party's perception is the other party's reality.

• *"Yes . . . really? . . . uh-huh . . . oh, that's interesting . . ."* Most people can be encouraged to share more information by simple verbal prompting along with encouraging body language like nods, smiles, and expressions that show you anticipate more to come. People like to talk to good listeners. Be a good listener (as discussed in chapter 2).

After they have answered, remain silent, as if you are expecting more. In negotiation, silence is normally a show of strength and experience. Not only that, but silence will usually cause the other party to speak. Their speaking gives you more information.

- *"Are there others involved, or do you make the final decision?"* This is a very good question near the beginning of a negotiation. Usually the other party's ego gets in their way and they say, "I make the final decision on these matters." Even if they don't have final authority, this effectively eliminates their ability to later claim that a third party needs to agree before action can be taken (see "Agent of Limited Authority," on page 159). If you feel this question may offend the other party, you can ask it in a less direct manner, such as, *"In matters like these, how are the final decisions made?"* (eliminating direct reference to the other party).

- *"I don't understand,"* or *"I'm not sure I understand."* These practically always work in getting more information.

- *"Do I know everything I should know in this matter?"* Put yourself in the position of the other party. This question will likely lead them to think, "What are you going to find out later that I should have shared when you asked that question?" This is one of the most powerful questions to ask in any negotiation. It's open-ended and normally elicits valuable information that wouldn't otherwise be available. It can be used anytime in the negotiation, and is particularly effective when you can't think of another question to ask but feel you don't have enough information to move forward.

3. To Give Information

In my seminars, I often ask this question, "Do you think anyone would ever ask a question to give information?" What does this do? Precisely what we are discussing. I asked a question that gave the information I wanted them to have. You should use this type of skillfully asked, information-giving question when you want to give the other party information they do not have.

• *"Bill, are you aware that if we took the course you are suggesting, we would both be opening ourselves to litigation?"* This type of question would be especially helpful when you think the other party might not be aware of an important fact, or if you feel it is necessary to remind them of it.

• *"Is there a possibility of . . . ?"* This simply provides the other party with a new option they would not otherwise have considered. Phrasing the question in this way also presents the option as a joint discovery.

• *"If we did this, wouldn't it be a big perk for your family?"*

• *"Wouldn't this plan avoid a lot of time and expense in the future?"* Of course, it obviously would—you simply want the other party to discover it, rather than stating it as an absolute fact.

• *"Can you guarantee this will be the lowest price available on this make and model? If not, I'll need to do some*

shopping before I make a decision." Note how the statement after the question makes the question particularly
powerful. You are letting them know that you have or
could have other alternatives. They need to get to the
bottom line before you leave and they lose the sale or
negotiation. It may even serve to let the person know
you have some negotiating savvy, saving both of you
time and energy.

4. To Buy Time or Stall

Experienced negotiators will sometimes ask a question
to buy some extra time. You might need more time to
think, or for any other reason that the passage of time
might work to your advantage. These sound very much
like information-gathering questions, but the motive is
different. It is possible that the same question will be
used to accomplish both purposes, each in its own situation. Simply ask the question and let the other party
talk. Any valuable information that comes forth while
you're using this time is simply a bonus.

Remember—the question must not appear to the
other party as a stalling technique. To do this, avoid asking about things unrelated to the negotiation, unless
you have a specific reason to ask (in which case, you
should be ready to share your reason).

• *"Could you explain that offer?"* Very often, an offer
will be modified when you ask to have it explained—and
virtually always, it is a change favorable to you.

• *"Tell me more about that."*

• *"What did you have in mind when you talked about . . . ?"*

• *"What would be the ideal situation for you?"* A great question to understand the real needs and wants of the other party. You may then want to share your "ideal situation" in the spirit of partnering.

• *"Could you repeat that offer?"* I remember my son, Ryan, placing an ad in the paper to buy a shotgun the year he turned old enough to hunt. He talked with someone by phone who offered to bring over a gun that he wanted to sell. Ryan did his homework and was prepared to pay $75 to $100 for the right gun. When the seller showed him the gun, it was just what he was looking for.

"Fifty dollars," the seller said.

"Fifty dollars?!" Ryan exclaimed, shocked that the price was that low.

"Well . . . okay, I'll take forty dollars cash for it right now."

It didn't take Ryan long to produce the forty dollars. And he learned a valuable lesson—always ask to have the offer repeated. Good negotiators often ask to have the offer repeated because many times the offer is changed in their favor (particularly if it is accompanied with a flinch—see page 187).

5. To Lead or Mold Thinking

Skillfully asked questions can move the other party's thinking in the exact direction you want it to go. Rather

than "telling" or "selling" the advantages of your proposal, you can use questions to let the other party discover them on their own. A "What if . . . ?" question can
be an excellent technique for leading the other party's
thinking. People love to be guided, but hate to be told
what to do. Here are some other examples:

• *"If you were in my position, what would you suggest?"*
This type of question uses the strategy of active participation (see page 184), or asking the other party to step
into your shoes. This is a great question to ask both an
empathetic person and someone whom you suspect
will *not* be comfortable looking at it from your point of
view.

• *"What would happen if we took this portion of your
proposal and this portion of my proposal and put them together like this?"* This is a great question. It takes some
of their ideas and some of your ideas and combines
them into a plan that, hopefully, you could both accept. The wording of that question patterns itself well
to the entire partnering approach outlined in the introduction (pages 1–16) by using portions of each party's proposal.

6. To Determine the Other Party's Position

In any negotiation, there are important questions that
can and should be used to determine where the other
party is in the negotiation process. It is, in a sense, getting information, but it is a specific type of information
(finding out how close they are to reaching an agree-

ment). Thus, it is separated from the other functions of questions.

• *"What would it take to . . . [make it work, close the deal, and accomplish both our needs]?"* This is a good question to ask near the end of a negotiation if things are stalled. Be careful not to back the other party into a corner. A question like, "Is that your final offer?" might do just that. Then there would be no way for them to continue to make concessions and still "save face."

• *"Which parts of the proposal [offer, deal, transaction] are most important to you?"* This is an excellent question to ask when you realize you will need to make concessions. It will help you determine which concessions will accomplish the most in satisfying the other party's needs and minimizing the "cost" to you.

• *"If we could put the deal together, where would you want to start [list the desirable answers]?"* Without forcing the other party to make a final commitment, this question gently moves them toward the result you are seeking. They see more clearly the completed deal.

• *"Is there a way we can get this done?"* An excellent question when you are stalled or at an apparent impasse.

• *"Where is there room for compromise?"* This is an excellent question to ask when you are at an impasse and can't find a good alternative. You are fishing for mutual gain. You might as well ask for it!

• *"If I could do [this] for you, could you do [that] for me?"* or *" . . . what could you do for me?"* A great question at an impasse, this conditional concession (see page 103) provides the opportunity for a win-win trade of concessions.

• *"What is your offer?"* When it is to your advantage to have the other party make the opening offer (see page 209), simply ask for it. Salespeople call these questions closing questions. They are questions most appropriately asked near the end of a negotiation when trying to determine whether the other party is close to reaching an agreement with you. They are questions such as:

- *"Would you want to special order or would the blue or gray we have in stock meet your needs?"*
- *"Would you need to take possession immediately or would fifteen days from closing be sufficient?"*
- *"Would you pay with cash, credit card, or would you prefer to finance?"*

• *"What is your thinking or rationale behind your proposal [or offer or position]?"* This question helps identify the real needs of the other party and separates those needs from their stated position. As chapter 12 will demonstrate, positions are much harder to satisfy than needs.

For example, the other party's position is, "We will not accept your offer." In an attempt to satisfy their position you might assume that it would help to (1) reduce the price, (2) concede additional services, or (3) lower the interest rate. The truth is, none of these satisfies their need, which is to get a lower down payment because of their current lack of cash. It could be easy to satisfy their needs if you ask the right question to draw it out from them. Satisfying the position is "hit or miss" if you don't take the time to find out the rationale behind it. If you don't ask, you might make costly concessions (price, extra services, and interest rates) in vain. In short, separate the position from the need. Questions like this one will help you do just that.

There are certainly other reasons to ask questions in a negotiation, but most of them fall into the six categories described above. This section has two main points. First, there are many reasons to ask questions in addition to just getting information. Be aware of them. Use them. Second, skilled negotiators spend a lot of negotiating time asking questions and probing for more information. In your next negotiation, pay particular attention to the amount of time you spend asking questions. Spend more time asking. Spend time crafting better questions.

Start building a list of questions that work for you in the type of negotiations you normally experience. Learn them so that they become natural. You will automatically and instinctively become better at asking questions. We might aptly restate Voltaire's quote to say: Judge a *negotiator* by his questions rather than by his answers. Skilled negotiators perfect their question-asking technique and constantly build their list of effective questions.

ALTERNATIVES TO ANSWERING
A QUESTION

We've examined the important process of asking questions in the negotiation, but what about the other side? If a good negotiator asks many questions, a great negotiator must be skilled at answering questions. Practically all of the time, you will provide a direct, complete answer. There are, however, a few occasions where the skilled negotiator chooses not to answer a question—at least not directly at the time the question is asked. You might not want to answer a question immediately for these reasons:

- You don't have enough information to answer correctly.
- You need time to formulate an answer that will support your position.
- A time delay in the negotiation works to your advantage.
- You need to supply the other party with more information so they will understand your position better.

Here are six creative options or alternatives when you wish to avoid answering a question.

1. Answer a Question with a Question

- *"That's an interesting question. Why do you ask?"*

- *"How would you like me to answer that question? I'm not sure what you are asking."* Notice how the statement following the question softens and clarifies the question's intention.

• *"Huh?"* or *"What?"* The advantage of a short, generic answer like one of these is that the pressure moves from you (when you are asked the initial question) to them (when you ask your short question). Appropriate use of these short questions is when you truly don't understand or you don't know what you don't know.

You might also ask a question specifically related to the content of the question asked, as in: "When you say 'problems,' are you referring to the problems before or after the modifications were made?" Or, "Do you have a copy of the appraisal? May I see it? If I became a serious buyer, would you mind my obtaining a second appraisal?"

2. Delay

• *"That's a good question and I want to answer it, but in order to make sense out of my answer, we need to discuss . . ."* You have the right to delay your answer to a question for just cause. For example, you might need to delay your response until you have provided additional facts or concepts, so that you know the answer will be understood. It is difficult to understand Algebra 3 when you have not taken Algebra 1 and 2.

3. Answer a Different Question
Sometimes this is called the "politician's technique" because we see it so much before election time. It goes like

this, *"That's a good question! What I hear you asking me is . . . ,"* and then the person proceeds to pose and answer the question *they* want to answer, not the one originally asked. I'm not suggesting you use that technique. I think it is manipulative and would not use it myself, but be aware of it—it might be used on you. When it is used on you, say, *"No, that's not the question I asked. What I asked was [repeat the question]."*

4. Refuse to Answer

Remember, you always have the right to say no. In order to maintain a positive partnering relationship with the other party, you could say, *"No, I can't answer that because . . ."*

- *". . . I don't know the answer."*
- *". . . It's an unfair question."* You would probably want to justify why it is unfair.
- *". . . It's confidential information."*

Don't be afraid to say no, but in order to maintain a positive relationship, provide the reason for not answering.

5. Ask to Have the Question Repeated or Explained

This is an excellent technique because skilled negotiators know that when you ask to have a question repeated, it often is changed in the process. Be sure you understand the question before you answer it. Don't hesitate to say, "I don't understand." Don't assume anything. It's better to appear uninformed than to assume that you know it all.

6. Remain Silent

We're all familiar with the phrase "Silence is golden" and this can be particularly true when a question is asked. Did you ever notice how the pressure swings when a question is asked? At first, all the pressure is on the person asked, but as the time goes on, the pressure gradually shifts. The longer the time without an answer, the more pressure builds on the person who asked the question. What normally happens? Usually the person asking the question will answer their own question or ask it again in a way that makes it easier to answer.

**"Remember not only to say the right thing
at the right time in the right place,
but far more difficult still, to leave unsaid the
wrong thing at the wrong moment."**
—Benjamin Franklin

2
Keys to Listening

We have two ears and one tongue
that we may hear more and speak less.
—Diogenes

Here is something you can take to the bank—find a great negotiator and you will have found a great listener. Asking the right questions is very important, but it's all for naught if you don't listen carefully and skillfully for the answers.

Dr. Lyman Steil is considered by many to be the world's foremost expert in the area of listening. His formula for effective listening is $L = (A \times W)^2$. Listening equals the quantity of ability times willingness squared. Ability and willingness, then, are the two factors that determine listening effectiveness. One without the other is exponentially less effective. Let's analyze both factors.

- *Listening ability* is a learned skill. It is something that can be improved with the knowledge and practice of listening techniques. The majority of this chapter will be devoted to examining and applying listening techniques.

- *Listening willingness*, on the other hand, is a function of one's motivation and desire. Without the desire or willingness to listen, our listening will be ineffective in spite of listening ability.

The motivation or willingness to listen does not come naturally to most people. Most would rather talk than listen. Here is the typical thought process: "If I can be persuasive in the things I say, I can convince the other party of what is needed to successfully complete this negotiation and therefore satisfy my needs." This is often faulty thinking for three reasons:

- You are going to waste a lot of time trying to convince the other party of things they already agree with or couldn't care less about.
- You are assuming that you know what they need to reach agreement. That assumption is usually wrong, or at best, incomplete.
- You will be so busy thinking about what you are going to say next that you won't concentrate on what the other party is saying.

Do as much research as you can before the negotiation begins to know the other party's needs. Once begun, your best research tool is listening, combined with effective questioning to further understand their needs. Meeting those needs is the key in most successful negotiations.

Now let's examine some of the primary techniques to increase listening ability.

1. Take the Predominant Responsibility in the Communication Process as the Listener

Act as if you have the lion's share of the responsibility for the success of the communication. This means that if you don't understand what the other party is saying, ask and get a clarification. Consider the communication process your personal responsibility and do what you need to do to assure that complete and effective communication takes place.

Often my audiences in a seminar or training program do a great job with this principle. They simply raise their hand and *ask* when they don't understand. I appreciate that! Despite the fact that I consider myself a good communicator, I often find that there are others in the audience who didn't understand either. Everyone wins. Understanding emerges from misunderstanding because a participant has taken the predominant responsibility as a listener.

2. Look for the Value Moments in Listening (VMLs)

Everyone comes to listening environments with a different background, different mind-set, and different perspective. As we listen, certain items become gems of information to us because they reveal important insights into the other party's needs. Dr. Steil calls these Value Moments in Listening, or VMLs. Good listeners are aware of these value moments and are constantly looking for them. See if you can pick up the VML in this statement: "I'm not sure that would work for us now, as we're about to change all of our tooling to meet the new government standards. This is particularly important to us in light of our budget cuts in all departments." There are two VMLs here that give potentially great insight into the current needs within the organization (changing tooling and budget cuts). Can you use that knowledge to meet both parties' needs? Even look behind their stated needs to the real needs. Read between the lines. Note *how* things are said as well as *what* is said. Read body language (see chapter 8). VMLs often become the key item of information that will determine the outcome of a negotiation.

I love to read my written evaluations following a workshop or seminar. One of the response items says, "The idea I found most helpful was ___." Almost every participant's response to that question is different, despite the fact that they all heard the same presentation. Why? It's simple . . . different value moments for different people. Good negotiators look for VMLs.

3. Take Notes
A good listener usually takes notes for several reasons:

- First, you are creating a permanent record. A negotiator takes control of a negotiation when she says, "According to my notes of our phone conversation on August 27 at 9:30 a.m., you said . . ." Notes provide an organized record of past conversations and that information is often the little difference that makes a big difference.
- Reducing things to writing helps to crystallize your thinking. Crystallized thinking helps you better understand the other party's needs. It also helps

you be more articulate in expressing your own
needs and what might be done mutually to bring
about agreement.

- Finally, educators tell us that even if we never refer
to our notes, we are much more likely to remember
things that we have written down.

I should mention here that there are two good reasons why, in some situations, you might not want to
take notes. The first is the importance of reading body
language, which is difficult to do while taking notes.
The second is the importance of maintaining eye contact. Eye contact says, "I'm interested!" and "I'm confident!" We'll discuss body language and eye contact in
detail in chapter 8. Remember to consider these two factors when deciding whether to take notes in a negotiation.

4. Plan to Report

One of the most powerful ways to improve listening
ability is to plan to report on what you heard. Even if
there is no one to report to, enlist someone (such as a
spouse, associate, or friend). Why are tests given in the
classroom? It's simple. Teachers and trainers realize that
people listen more attentively when they have to report.
Whenever you want to listen more attentively, plan to
report.

5. When Distractions Occur, Return to the Content

Distractions become a primary reason for the lack of effective listening. Some people are more prone to this

than others. Good listeners are preconditioned so that when a distraction occurs, they immediately return to the content of the communication. Typical distractions include peculiarities in the other person's speech, dress, or mannerisms; lighting, noise, or movement distractions; preoccupations or worries; or lack of interest in what is being discussed. Good listeners in a negotiation situation have a mind-set that causes them to be alert to these distractions and to return their attention immediately to the content.

6. Identify and Utilize Communication Style or Structure

Most people, by nature, tend to prefer structure in their communication. As a skilled listener, identify that style early in the communication process and use it to better understand the other party by knowing how you expect them to structure their thoughts. Not only will you more quickly understand the other party (because you understand their preference in communication style), but you will also be more effective with them because you can use their style in communicating with them. Examples of communication styles include the following:

Enumeration

This is simply the developing of lists or numerically ordered items. You may have already noted that I have a strong tendency to communicate via this method. Thus, much of the material presented throughout this book is done through enumeration. You understand me better because you know what to expect. Not only that, but you would use enumeration, when possible, in communicating with me because it is my style of choice and I best understand ideas and concepts presented that way. The same two benefits (better understanding of the other party and more effective communication with the other party) apply to the next two communication styles.

Problem—Cause—Effect—Solution

Many people use this logical communication path for presenting their ideas. For example, "Our problem of . . . is caused by . . . resulting in . . . and we can solve this problem by . . ."

Spatial/Pictorial

Some people like to paint a visual picture when they talk, similar to what an artist does on canvas. When the skilled listener hears these visual descriptions, she can shift her normal listening style to using her powers of visualization to aid in understanding. She may then choose to describe things visually, since she sees that is the other's preference.

7. Identify and Cater to Cultures and Traditions

Any way you look at it, a person's personal, social, and political background can play a large part in the communication process. Emotions, both positive and negative, are triggered by three major sources:

- People (race, color, creed, national origin, age, sex, etc.)

- Issues (politics, religion, welfare, immigration, etc.)
- Language (regional and national accents, pronunciations, soft and loud speaking, etc.)

A good listener is uniquely aware of the various items in each of these areas that trigger either positive or negative responses in both themselves and the other party. As I have traveled in many different countries, I've become aware of the unique customs, traditions, and mannerisms of various cultures. Obviously, these affect the method of negotiating. One of the most helpful tools to learn more about the country in which you are traveling is a CultureGram, a brief four- to six-page report providing key facts that a foreigner should know about the country in which they are traveling or doing business. They are available at www.culturegrams.com or call 800-521-3042.

Do not think this chapter's brevity implies anything about its importance. Remember the primary point:

The motivation to listen is the single most important factor in increasing your listening effectiveness.

I encourage you to master the seven important listening techniques above and to resolve to listen more intently in your next negotiation. Many readers and seminar participants have reported that this section on listening has helped them be more effective in every other area of the negotiating process as well. I promise that your negotiating ability will increase greatly as your motivation to listen increases, and with it your ability to listen. Notice that increased effectiveness, and your motivation to listen will increase even more.

"If I listen, I have the advantage.
If I speak, others have it."

—Unknown

3
Power Factors

*If you are going to fight, don't let them talk you
into negotiating.
But, if you are going to negotiate, don't let them talk you
into fighting.*
—Abraham Lincoln

Once needs are established (through questioning and
listening), the next step is to determine the power of
each party. Understanding the ten power factors is critical in this process. These factors lay the groundwork for
negotiation planning. If you don't know who has the
power and why, you're lost before you begin. Knowing
these factors, you can determine the power of the other
party and maximize your own power. In the description
of each factor, you will learn through examples how to
use that power factor to your advantage. With this
knowledge of power, the remaining chapters of the book
will give you the tools necessary to successfully conclude your negotiations. You can adjust your negotiating
strategy based on these factors.

Occasionally in negotiations, some of the factors
affecting power will be "givens"—that is, they will
not be under your control. However, it is a rare negotiation where one or more of these factors does not

yield significant power to its user. Know and understand them all.

ALTERNATIVE POWER

Nothing increases your power in a negotiation more than having good, viable alternatives. Never enter a negotiation without having at least one strong alternative to the current negotiation. In other words, what are you going to do if you don't come to an agreement with this party?

Example: You are buying a new car. The dealership near your home has the exact vehicle you want—color, style, and all the accessories right down to the onboard navigation system. They have the best service department in the area—an important factor to you. Your spouse is ecstatic about the car. Perfect negotiation scenario, right? Wrong!

You're giving yourself no alternatives, plus your want is too great. This puts you in the worst possible negotiation position. Here are some practical alternatives:

- Call the next closest dealership and explain your situation—you were planning to buy the vehicle at your local dealership but you heard that this one often gives some amazing deals. You wanted to check them (and another dealership) out before making a final decision. Wouldn't even a very small profit look good to the second dealership that now has an immediate potential sale come unexpectedly?

- Approach a local dealership that is most competitive with the vehicle you really want. Use the same procedure as above.
- Go online and search for the vehicle that is exactly (or almost) what you want. Get a price quote.

Armed with the above three options (and perhaps more that you've researched), you are prepared to approach the original dealership with some realistic alternatives. You are not at their mercy. You don't absolutely need *their* vehicle.

Another example: Consider what the National Football League management did in responding to the players' demands and subsequent strike many years ago. They developed a creative alternative—they signed other ball players to what many dubbed "scab" or "scrub" teams and were able to play the scheduled games despite the strike by the regular players. Good alternative? I don't know . . . but it sure gave them power in that negotiation. Management came out on top because they were able to show the players on strike that they had an alternative.

Never enter a negotiation without at least one good alternative!

LEGITIMACY POWER

Legitimacy power can be a major factor in the outcome of any negotiation. It's often referred to as credibility. What causes a company, organization, or individual to have legitimacy? At least three factors contribute. Use them to your advantage as you prepare for any negotiation.

Track Record or Performance Power

It's hard to argue with success. A track record or outstanding past performance unquestionably builds credibility. How can you demonstrate your track record to the other party? It will be different for each negotiation, but an essential part of the planning process.

Example: You are aware that all alternatives for the other party involve substantial risk. You plan your strategy to emphasize early in the negotiation how risk-free your alternative is, perhaps even asking (if it's not obvious) how this compares with their other options.

Another example: It never ceases to amaze me how many organizations are willing to hire me as a speaker based on my having spoken to certain other organizations. They know the screening process these other organizations go through in selecting their speakers!

Do you think I use that to my advantage? You had better believe I do! How? I might underscore it by saying something like this: "When I spoke to the XYZ organization, I used [this technique]. Do you think that would work for your group also?"

Referral Power

What other people are saying can also contribute greatly to your legitimacy.

Example: Seeking the endorsement of well-known celebrities is an effective advertising technique that puts billions of dollars in the hands of advertisers and millions in the hands of celebrities each year. On a lesser scale, an endorsement from the CEO of a reputable relevant company, or of anyone who is known and respected in a similar field or endeavor, can build legitimacy for the recipient.

Another example: *Consumer Reports* is considered by many to be one of the top independent sources of information about products and services. Hypothetically, let's assume you were considering buying a car and you initially preferred a Lexus. You might be persuaded to reconsider if a person selling a Lincoln directed you to an issue of *Consumer Reports* that compared both makes, feature for feature, and the Lincoln was reported clearly superior. If the salesperson had simply asserted the same claims without providing independent evidence, you would be far less likely to reconsider.

Title Power

Use your title, degree, designation, or accomplishments to add to your legitimacy.

- An office or position, such as President, CEO, CFO, General Manager, Chairman of the Board, VP of Sales
- An academic degree or accomplishment, such as PhD, MBA, BS, BA, MS, MA, MD, DDS
- A license, such as CPA or RN

- An award or honor, such as Pulitzer Prize, Olympic Gold Medal, Outstanding Salesman Award, Million-Dollar Round Table, Businessman of the Year Award

Aside from showing the above "titles" in a written form, you can also subtly work them into conversations, as in these examples:

- "That happened the same year I made the Million-Dollar Round Table."
- "She said, 'Dr. Hennig, could I ask you a question?'"
- "As CFO of the organization, it was my responsibility to . . ."

In my small organization, we have had such impressive titles as Vice President of Sales, Office Manager, and National Coordinator. Why? Because these titles provide legitimacy. One day my assistant told me the Walt Disney organization had called inquiring about a possible negotiation program. I was out, so she returned the call. "This is Shirley Moore, Dr. Hennig's National Coordinator."

Bam! She was transferred immediately to the VP who had called and booked the date. Why? Partly based on her "legitimate" title.

Do everything you can to build your legitimacy power.

RISK POWER

The amount of risk either party can afford to take (or is willing to take) greatly affects who has the power (and how much they have) in a negotiation.

Example: Compare these two situations. In the first, the owners of a large corporation decide on an asking price for a division of their company and determine that they can reduce that price in negotiations by only 4 percent to reach a negotiated agreement. In another scenario, the owners agree that they can reduce the price by as much as 15 percent because it is imperative that they sell the division within three months.

The owners in the first scenario are willing to take a greater risk. Their small bargaining range means the division may not sell. But since they are willing to take that risk, they are much more likely to receive a higher price than the owners in the second situation are. In short, the willingness to take a risk greatly enhances the owners' negotiating position. They may not consummate the sale, but if they do, it will likely be at a much higher price.

Another example: I enjoy demonstrating risk power to my seminar participants. I give each audience member ten-to-one odds in their favor, on a fifty-fifty coin flip. Here is how it works:

If they call the coin flip correctly, I give them $1,000,000 cash. If they call it incorrectly, they owe me $100,000 (I do hasten to point out that this is a hypothetical situation!). Then I ask, "If the offer was real, and

I had the cash ready to deliver, how many of you would take me up on the deal?"

Less than 10 percent of those in my audiences take me up on the offer.

Why? It's certainly not because they don't want $1,000,000. Nor is it that the odds are not good. It's simply because they can't afford to take the *risk*. Imagine having to get the spouse on the phone and explain that they had to come up with $100,000! It wouldn't matter to the spouse that it was ten-to-one odds on a fifty-fifty flip.

Then I change the situation slightly.

"Let's change only the dollar amounts—ten dollars to you if you call it correctly, one dollar to me if you call it incorrectly."

I always get 100 percent of the group taking me up on that deal! The difference? They could *afford* to take a one-dollar risk.

I often have two people come up to me at the break and say, "We've changed our minds and we are both going to take you up on the $1,000,000 coin flip—he is heads and I am tails!"

What did they do? Very simply, they found a way to reduce their risk (in this case down to 0 percent). If it weren't hypothetical, they would have $900,000 to split between them.

The same is true in any negotiation—the person who is able to take the most risk has the most power in that negotiation. Now, I am not suggesting that you take more risks. That is a decision you will have to make. However,

I will tell you this: the more risk you can (or are willing to) take in a negotiation, the more power you have.

Many experienced negotiators have shared with me that risk power was the most important information they learned from my seminars, books, or CDs, saying, "I used to close eight out of ten deals. Now I close only seven out of ten. But my profitability on the seven is so much better than on the eight that I am much more profitable."

The more risk you can afford to take (or are willing to take), the more power you have in a negotiation.

Another example: A young friend approached me wanting help in negotiating to buy his family's first home. He felt that a few good negotiating tips might save him several thousand dollars. The seller was asking $150,000 for the home. I asked him how he felt about the price.

"That's fantastic, it's really a bargain." He pointed out his family had been looking for a home like this for years and hadn't found one. He said they were considering building a home, and didn't think they could build one they liked any more than this one. I asked him what it would cost to build.

About $225,000, he told me.

I asked him what would happen if someone else bought the home that afternoon.

"That would be a disaster!"

He had two viable options:

- Buy the home immediately. This would allow him
  to take advantage of a $75,000 savings over his
  BATNA (best alternative to negotiated agreement;
  see page 82), building a similar home ($225,000 –
  $150,000 = $75,000).
- Attempt to negotiate for a better price than $150,000
  (say $140,000), which, if successful, would allow
  my friend to take advantage of an $85,000 savings
  over his BATNA.

My advice to him? It was not worth risking a $75,000
savings for the possibility of an additional $10,000.

COMMITMENT POWER

It is very important here to differentiate the two types of
commitment: the commitment to reach an agreement
and the commitment to your position.

Commitment to reach *an agreement* is important for
both parties. But as the great negotiator Herb Cohen says,
"You've got to want it . . . but not too much." This definitely applies to our desire to reach an agreement of some
kind. If reaching an agreement is a necessity for you, obviously you are in a weaker position (assuming the other
party is aware of that fact). Try not to be too committed
(or at least not to appear too committed) to reaching an
agreement.

On the other hand, the stronger your demonstrated
commitment to *your position* is, the more power you
have.

Remember, there may be a difference between *real*

commitment and *demonstrated* commitment. The other party may have only a slight need to remain firm on their initial offer, but if they demonstrate a firm commitment to that position, they gain power in the negotiation. You say to yourself, "Wow! They sure sound committed to their position. We may not be able to get what we thought we could get here." You begin lowering your expectations. In short, one party gains power by sending a message to the other party that they have a firm commitment behind their position. How strong a commitment to your position you choose to demonstrate is a decision only you can make.

The more committed you are to your position, the stronger position you are in. Remember, however, that a strong commitment maintained to the end of the negotiation may result in no agreement, so if you take this approach, be prepared to risk walking away from the deal.

Example: Let's return to the NFL player/management negotiation we discussed on page 45. At the beginning of that negotiation, the players had a strong commitment to their position—they were unified and firm. As the season began, and the "scab" teams began playing regular season games, many players realized that their salaries for those games would never be recovered. It began to hurt their wallets badly. Gradually, more and more players rejoined their teams, thus demonstrating considerably less commitment to the players' negotiating position. Commitment power became an important determinant in the outcome of that negotiation. The amount of commitment demonstrated can play a major factor in your negotiating success.

KNOWLEDGE POWER

Knowledge is power in a negotiation. The more you know, the more power you possess. Three areas are particularly important: knowing the topic, the negotiation process, and the other party's situation.

Topic Knowledge

Even a skilled negotiator is ineffective when they fail to fully understand the topic they are negotiating.

If it's real estate—study real estate.

If it's automobiles—study automobiles.

If it's construction—study construction.

If it's accounting—study accounting.

If you aren't knowledgeable about the topic/product you're negotiating on, get help from an expert who is.

Negotiations Knowledge

Knowledge of the negotiation process itself is key, specifically, for example:

- Strategies and tactics and their counters
- Alternatives for overcoming an impasse
- Effective questioning techniques
- Guidelines for concessions
- Team negotiating techniques

Reading and practicing the suggestions in this book will give you negotiation knowledge and thus power.

Other Party Knowledge

Simply put, the more you know about the other party and their situation, the more power you have. Specific knowledge of the other party that will help you includes:

- Personality style
- Behavioral characteristics
- Negotiating habits, likes, and dislikes
- Needs, wants, and desires for this specific negotiation
- Their alternatives if they don't reach agreement with you

There are two primary ways to gather knowledge about the other party: (1) do as much research as possible before the negotiation, and (2) ask the right questions (see chapter 1) and listen carefully to the answers (see chapter 2).

EXPERT POWER

If you don't have knowledge power, use expert power.

Example: My office manager used expert power to her advantage several years ago. She had been in an accident that totaled her car, and the insurance adjuster was coming that day to settle the claim. She told me she was not a good negotiator and asked if I'd sit in so she wouldn't be taken. She said she knew very little about car values so she asked her automobile dealer friend to sit in also. Put yourself in the position of the insurance adjuster. He quickly realized that Linda had on her team a negotiation expert and an automobile price expert. I said very little. The auto dealer said very little. The adjuster was in no mood for an argument with two experts. Linda quickly got a great settlement. She lacked knowledge power but compensated by using expert power.

REWARD (OR PUNISHMENT) POWER

Dr. Jim Tunney, past president of the National Speakers Association and a former National Football League referee, tells a great story demonstrating reward power. At a banquet where he was set to deliver an after-dinner address, he asked the waiter for an extra pat of butter. The waiter said, "One pat of butter per customer."

Well, you'd think that wouldn't be a great negotiation challenge for Tunney, who dealt with big football players every weekend. He thought, "How can I negotiate an extra pat of butter from this waiter?" The thought came to him, "This guy doesn't know who I am." So Jim said, "Sir, do you know who I am?"

"No."

"I'm the guy who has to speak to all these thousands of people out here!"

The waiter did not look very impressed. "Sir, do you know who *I* am?"

"No," said a startled Tunney.

"I'm the guy in charge of the butter!"

Despite lacking most of the other factors, the waiter had the ability to reward or punish and it gave him great power. This is an example of how not to use power! Occasionally you will have to do things to which people will take offense. Be careful not to use power in a petty way, just because you can. Remember you want to build relationships so people want to continue to work with you.

Another example: An executive approached a speaker she was considering booking for a breakout session at her association's annual convention. After considerable discussion, the exec told the speaker she would continue her search and be back in touch with her in a week or two.

Thinking quickly, the speaker asked, "Are there any other spots you're seeking to fill with professional speakers?"

"Yes, we were hoping to get [a certain speaker] as our opening keynoter and [a certain other speaker] as our closing keynoter."

"I know them both personally, and have shared the platform with them many times. Perhaps I could be of assistance."

The speaker, weak though her position may have been in influencing the exec to hire her, had thrown out a potential "reward" just at the right time. It balanced out her weaker position. It was hard for the exec not to hire her after she persuaded both of the bigger name speakers to fit into the association's limited budget. Even when in a weak position, look for situations that give you the ability to reward or punish.

TIME (OR DEADLINE) POWER

In virtually any negotiation, the party who has a dead-line loses power. When you have to make something happen on a tight deadline, often the only thing that you can do is make concessions (see chapter 4). If, on the other hand, time is of no consequence to you, you have no pressing needs and no reason to have to take immediate action.

Example: I'm surprised how many times I've experienced the same response from a seminar participant at the break following a discussion of deadline power. The story usually goes like this:

"I'm the person in our firm responsible for the negotiating we do in Japan. When I travel there for the negotiation, the first thing they determine is the time of my return flight to the States. Then they entertain me well, but negotiations seem to be delayed until close to my return deadline. Then who makes the concessions? I do!"

Do whatever possible in a negotiation to avoid having a deadline. If you have a deadline, try not to reveal it. It is an appropriate confidential item. Another way to handle this situation would be to have reason (as an "important" meeting with someone back home in your own company) for an earlier departure date. Then, if you need the extra time to be effective in the negotiation, you can, at the last minute, cancel the "important" meeting and change your flight. For this maneuver, you need to have bought a refundable ticket, which costs a bit more, but its cost is more than made up by your ability to conduct an effective negotiation.

Be aware of the other party's deadlines. Do your research before the negotiation. Ask questions. Listen carefully to the answers. Your knowledge and tactful use of these deadlines can provide great power for you.

PERCEPTION POWER

It is not who has the power but who is perceived *to have the power that really matters.*

Example: Let's use the first power factor we discussed, alternative power. Assume I have absolutely no alternatives in my negotiation with you. You are the only source for me to accomplish what I hope to accomplish. But for some reason you perceive that I have other alternatives. In this situation, it's just as if I have those alternatives, at least as far as this negotiation is concerned.

I'm not suggesting that you deceive the other party into believing you have power that you don't have. What I am saying is that if you have the power, but the other party doesn't know you have that power, it's just as if you don't have it. It does you absolutely no good. It is your job to skillfully inform the other party that you have that power.

Example: For the last four years you have been rated number one in customer satisfaction by J. D. Power and Associates but your potential customer is unaware of that fact. Here are several ways to let them know without just telling them directly (which is, of course, an option you may choose to use):

- Share a piece of literature on which that fact is clearly expressed.
- Send an e-mail that has a brief mention of that fact in the company information below your signature line.
- Build it into the conversation. ("Since I joined the company four years ago, we have been recognized by J. D. Power and Associates as . . .")

Be careful not to perceive more power in the other party than they actually possess. Research and know the other party before the negotiation. Ask! Ask! Ask during the negotiation. Knowledge is a big key to great negotiating. Get credit for all the power you possess. Don't overestimate the other party's power. It is not who has the power but who is *perceived* to have the power that really matters.

RELATIONSHIP (OR PARTNERING) POWER

I believe relationship power to be the most important factor in many negotiations today—yet twenty years ago it was hardly on my list! With each passing year, I believe it becomes more important. This is particularly true in longer negotiations, or when continuing negotiations are necessary with the same party. The eight partnering principles outlined in the introduction provide the best guidelines for building relationships. Additional ideas and examples appear in chapter 6, "Handling Difficult Negotiators," and chapter 12, "Avoiding Common Errors."

When the relationship is right, details rarely get in the way. When the relationship is not right, no amount of skilled negotiation will bring about agreement.

PART 2

Be Ready for Anything

Bumps in the road you are sure to encounter, and how to handle them with ease

4
Getting and Giving Concessions

Life cannot subsist in society
but by reciprocal concessions.
—Samuel Johnson

After having determined needs through good questions (chapter 1) and effective listening (chapter 2), and after understanding the balance of power (chapter 3), we move to the next step in negotiating: How can we ask for, and get, the concessions we seek? How can we make reasonable concessions ourselves without giving up the entire ship? How can we make the other party feel good in this challenging process?

Getting *and* giving concessions plays a critical role in most negotiations. I have been involved in thousands of negotiations, simulated and actual. Through my experience, I am convinced that there are certain principles or guidelines that can help anyone to be more effective in this process. You will be convinced also, as you apply these guidelines. Pay particular attention to the psychology behind each one. This gives you a deeper understanding of the guideline itself and a better feel for when and how to use it. For instance, two psychological principles lie behind the first guideline below, on giving yourself room to make concessions: (1) if you start high (or low) you both reduce the other party's expectation and give yourself room to make concessions, and (2) people like to receive concessions and are more likely to make a concession themselves after receiving one. The latter is particularly useful when you are negotiating with someone who expects to get concessions as a normal part of the negotiating process. Good negotiators know how to do it. Great negotiators know why they do it.

1. Give Yourself Room to Make Concessions

Your opening offer is a key component in any negotiation and has a direct correlation to the outcome. It should be as high (or low) as it can possibly be *without being perceived as unrealistic*. An apparently unrealistic high (or low) offer can be shown to be realistic by supporting it with sound, logical reasoning and facts.

Example: You are interested in purchasing a certain property with an asking price of $495,000. You say to the seller:

"Researching your property, I noticed that it has been on the market for six months without an offer. Wanting to make a realistic offer, I did some further research, and . . . "

"Here's a property, similar to yours in location, square footage, and layout that sold last month for $375,000 . . . "

"Here's another property with similar specifications that recently sold for $389,000 . . . "

"In addition, I would have to spend at least $55,000 to get a new roof, replace the central air-conditioning unit, and resurface the driveway."

"Given these facts, I'm prepared to pay $385,000 for this property."

That "unrealistic" low offer (when compared to the asking price) became realistic when backed up with recent sales of comparative properties and pointing out improvements that were necessary on the property.

In thousands of simulated negotiations in my live seminars, I find a direct correlation between the opening offer and the final agreement; the higher the opening offer, the higher the final agreement; the lower the opening offer, the lower the final agreement.

The experienced negotiator positions the initial offer so that concessions can be made without getting below their "walk-away" position. Prior to the first meeting with the other party, determine three key positions:

- *Your "Wish" Position*—the highest expectation you could reasonably achieve
- *Your "Best Guess" Position*—where you think you are most likely to agree
- *Your "Walk-Away" Position*—where it is better for you to walk away than to agree

These positions may change when you learn new facts in the process of the negotiation. *But an important word of caution—don't be too quick to lower your expectations in the heat and excitement of the negotiation.* Most people do not think clearly under pressure. Yes, you want to consummate the deal, but remember, you spent important, nonpressured thinking time to determine your three positions. Don't blow it with a quick, emotional change of heart that you may regret later.

2. Don't Make the First Concession on a Major Item

If you have time on your side, don't make the first concession, *period*. (See "Forbearance," page 162.) This always works to your advantage. Time is power (see page 58). As you feel the necessity to begin making concessions, choose small concessions that cost you little but have a highly perceived value to the other party. And, even before offering any concessions, ask: "If I could do *x* for you . . . could you do *y* for me?" or ". . . what could you do for me?"

Notice in the first question, you have something specific you want and you ask for it. In the second question, you ask an open-ended question. You will often be pleasantly surprised at what is offered with an open-ended question, but if the result is not agreeable, you can counter with the request for a specific concession. Either question may accomplish two important things:

- You may get something good that you didn't expect.
- The other party will realize that every time they ask for something, they are going to get asked for something in return. Eventually their requests for concessions will diminish or go away completely.

Example: Here is the scenario:

- There are three items that are critically important for you to obtain in this negotiation—A, B, and C.
- Four other items—B1, B2, B3, and B4—are important, but less critical.
- Three other items—C1, C2, and C3—are "red herrings," things that you don't want or need but might have value to the other side.

If you feel you should make a concession, use one or more of your "C" items first. As the negotiation proceeds, slowly move up the line, trying not to make concessions on your "A" items.

3. One of the Best Times to Get a Concession Is When You Are Asked for One

Stated another way: don't give a concession without asking for one in return, even if the concession is just a "brownie point" to be cashed in at a later time. The law of reciprocity comes into play here—people expect value for value. Use one of the two questions in guideline 2 above. Capitalize on basic human nature and remember . . . the best time to get a concession is when one is asked of you. While it may seem that guidelines 2 and 3 are making the same point, they are fundamentally different. Two is referring to something you should not do. Three is referring to something you should do.

4. Rarely Accept the First Offer

Getting some concessions is possible with practically every negotiator. Begin every negotiation by saying to yourself, "Every negotiator will concede something!" About 99 percent of the time, you will be right. By not accepting the first offer and creatively probing for areas where concessions may be made, you open your mind and, hopefully, the mind of the other party, to every possibility. Remember my negotiation maxim: If you don't ask for it, you will never get it.

Here are just a few things people commonly ask for and get at no cost to them:

- Hotel room upgrades
- A lower interest rate on their credit card
- Some furniture thrown in with a house purchase
- Accessories free with a vehicle purchase
- Airline upgrades
- Employer-paid health care in negotiating an employment contract
- Part or all of the closing costs on a home

As the old saying goes, the worst someone can say is no. I challenge you to ask for something you wouldn't normally ask for in your next negotiation. Just try it. Almost everything is negotiable. Then write and tell me about it.

5. Make People Work for Their Concessions

Let's assume you've just placed a classified ad in the paper to sell your car. A potential buyer responds immediately and, after a quick look at the car, offers to buy it for the price you are asking. You complete the deal and have the cash in your hand. You're happy, right? Wrong. You're likely to say to yourself: "I didn't ask for enough! I left several thousand dollars on the table. They would have paid me much more. Why did I ask for so little?"

Let's analyze this situation. If people immediately get the price they wanted, they feel they didn't ask enough. So if you want to keep the other party happy—and you always do in a negotiation—make them work for their concessions. For example, what an experienced buyer would do is to point out some minor problems (tires with thin tread, small scratches and door dents, spots on the carpet, etc.). Then they could ask (and would likely get) some small concession in price. The seller would be more satisfied with the transaction (even though they receive less for their car) and would not feel that they had left money on the table.

6. Avoid Concession-Making Patterns

Skilled negotiators not only avoid patterns in their own concessions, but also watch carefully for patterns in the other party's concessions.

Example: I was using an out-of-state law firm to settle a case that was domiciled in that state. We were very far apart in our opening offers. My attorney said, "Don't worry. This firm has a habit of waiting until two or three days before court is scheduled before making any concessions. Then they make a series of large, rapid concessions to avoid going to court."

Obviously, I preferred not to go to court, and with

that knowledge decided to buy a refundable airline ticket and hold tight, also making no concessions. Sure enough, three days before the court date, my attorney called with a significantly better offer. We gave a reasonable counteroffer that was accepted, saving us a good sum of money plus my time and travel expense. All of this was accomplished by a good attorney who knew enough to look for concession-making patterns in all of his business dealings.

When you are negotiating with the same party more than once, look for any patterns that may be a part of their negotiating style. It will enable you to capitalize on that knowledge, just as I did in the example above, because I knew they would be making concessions a few days before the court date. Equally important, don't allow yourself to fall into patterns of concession making that may be easily read and used to your disadvantage, as in the examples below.

Common Patterns In Concession Making
- *Lowballing or highballing:* asking for a large concession in hopes of getting the most possible. (See page 175.)
- *Using a piece of the pie (or the salami) technique:* asking for little things that individually may be small but collectively add up to a great deal. (See page 161.)
- *Padding:* building into an initial proposal items that they can concede (items they don't expect to get anyway).

- *Adding the nibble at the end:* asking for a concession at the time of closing that is so small it is likely to be included. (See page 169.)
- *Making assumptions:* acting as though concessions have been (or will be) made and moving on. (See "Act and Take the Consequences," page 170.)
- *Becoming an agent of limited authority:* setting things up so that concessions cannot be made without the approval of higher authority. (See page 159.)

7. Keep Concessions Small, Make Them Slowly, and Make Each One Progressively Smaller

Let's assume a seller is negotiating a product or service for which they are asking $10,000. Examine two different scenarios:

- Scenario 1: After a brief negotiation, a quick concession is made to $9,500, then to $9,000, then to $8,500.
- Scenario 2: After a long negotiation, a reluctant concession is made to $9,800, then to $9,700, then to $9,650.

In each case, three concessions were made. But in scenario 2, they were smaller concessions, made much more slowly, and each was made progressively smaller than the previous one. Don't you just get the feeling that in scenario 2 the negotiator is close to their bottom line? They may not be, but you might perceive that they are on the basis of the timing and amount of their concessions. In negotiation, perception often becomes reality. Use this fact to your advantage.

8. Don't Assume You Know What the Other Party Wants for Concessions

It would amaze most people to know how much they actually give away without having to, just because *they think they know* what the other party wants. Just because something was important to your last client (business associate, etc.) does not mean it is important to this one. *Don't assume! Ask! Ask! Ask!*

Make it a rule to never concede anything before you are absolutely sure it will make a positive difference that is worth the cost. Rather than assuming what the other party wants, here are some good questions to pose:

- "Which one of those items is most important to you?"
- "Which one is least important?"
- "If you were in my shoes, what would you suggest?"
- "What do you think is the best way to make this come together right now?"
- "Tell me more about your needs in this situation."
- "How can I best meet your needs and still make it reasonable for me?"

So many times we give more than is necessary. Probe before making concessions. Find out what the other party really wants.

9. Try to Determine All Requests Before Making Any Concessions

In an effective negotiating strategy called "a piece of the pie" (sometimes called "salami," see page 161), the negotiator asks for very small concessions, one at a time, and ends up with the "whole pie." This is why a good negotiator always tries to determine all requests before granting any concessions. Here is the ideal question that you should ask when confronted with any request for a concession (no matter how small):

"In addition to that, is there anything else you need before we close the deal [or sign the agreement, complete the paperwork, etc.]?"

This question actually accomplishes two purposes:

- It forces the other party to reveal their entire agenda before you make that concession.
- It effectively eliminates their later use of the piece of the pie technique because the other party soon learns that, when they ask for something, they will always be asked this question in return.

You may want to paste this valuable question on your bathroom mirror or refrigerator until it becomes automatic. It will save you big dollars in "concession giveaways" in the future. Practice makes perfect!

10. Don't Make a Counteroffer to an Unrealistic Offer

Most experienced negotiators simply refuse to begin until the starting point falls within a reasonable range. The philosophy here is that there is no reason to make a concession of any kind when you are so far from an offer that could bring about agreement. Refusal to move forward with the negotiation in this way is risky, but often very powerful. It saves time. Either the other party concedes, moving the negotiation forward, or the negotiation is terminated.

Example: Living in Wisconsin and planning an eventual move to Arizona, I was approached by a neighbor with some interest in buying my house. He asked what I wanted for it. I had done some research but not much.

"Gee, I don't know," I said. "I haven't really thought about it."

He quickly made me an offer.

"Oh, no," I said. "I know that is considerably below what I could consider."

He quickly came back to me with a significantly higher offer. My response was the same.

To make a long story short, he came back to me several times, each time with a higher offer. By then, I had researched and talked with a realtor friend to determine the actual value of the house. When my neighbor got within a reasonable price range, we began serious negotiations. I was in a much stronger position because I had simply, but kindly, backed away from the unrealistic offers.

It is better to back away or ignore an unrealistic offer until the other party brings the offer into a reasonable negotiating range.

---

11. Remember Relative Value

The skilled negotiator remembers the concept of relative value: what can you concede that costs you little in time or money but has high value to the other side?

Examples:

- The retailer who provides a one-year warranty on an appliance. The customer sees this as a big selling point, and yet the retailer knows from experience that their out-of-pocket costs in fulfilling the warranty are minimal.
- The automobile dealer who offers to throw in an accessory with a high retail value but very low wholesale cost to them.
- The manufacturer who concedes several months' free storage because they have two huge warehouses vacant.
- The accounting firm that concedes some free computer time to a potential new client in conjunction with a large one-year contract they're attempting to close (because they have a computer which is not used to full capacity and it costs them nothing to have this potential client use it at the times they are not using it).

The examples are endless. When making or seeking concessions, remember relative value.

Compromise is an absolutely essential element in the art of negotiation. Knowing and applying these principles will go a long way in helping you concede and get

concessions effectively. Remember they are principles—
not rules. They work in some situations—not all. Learn
them. Practice them. Then rely on your "gut" to apply
them in the "right" situations.

**"All government—indeed, every human benefit
and enjoyment, every virtue and every prudent
act—is founded on compromise and barter."**
—Edmund Burke

5
Negotiating from a Weak Position

Negotiations between conflicting parties is like
crossing a river by walking on slippery rocks . . .
It's risky, but it's the only way to get across.
—Hubert Humphrey

Like it or not, sometimes we find ourselves in a weak negotiating position. No one enjoys being in a weak
position—except the *really great negotiators*. They welcome
the opportunity as a personal challenge. Learn from
them. You, too, can become a master at negotiating from
a weak position. Every chapter of this book contains valuable information that is helpful when you are in a weak
position. Like a piece of a puzzle, every chapter helps us
see the bigger negotiation picture. The six key suggestions
here deal specifically with strategies to offset a weak position.

1. Avoid Defensiveness: Keep a Positive Attitude
One of the most costly errors in negotiation is underesti-
mating your own power. Your position, in many cases, is
not as weak as you think. Why? For starters, you are
fully aware of your own limitations. The other party is

probably not aware of them, at least not all of them. Likewise, you are aware of their strengths, but probably not aware of their limitations.

With these thoughts in mind, a positive mental attitude can go a long way in strengthening a weak position. Great negotiators believe they can overcome, and usually they do.

"No one can make you feel inferior without your consent."—Eleanor Roosevelt

---

2. Use "Partnering" Terminology and Philosophy

Remember the eight partnering principles described in the introduction and use them to strengthen your weak position:

- Act as if the relationship will last forever
- Understand needs and wants—the other party's and your own
- Adopt a "they," not "you," orientation
- Recognize feelings as facts
- Take no personal offense
- Use your power to build relationships
- Have honest, open communications
- Determine ahead of time how to resolve differences

Additionally, always begin the negotiation with statements that lay the groundwork for a positive environment.

Example: "Dan, I enjoy working with you because

you always seem to be able to put yourself in my shoes and we always seem to come out with a mutually beneficial solution. I want you to know that's my goal also. I really want to learn your needs in this situation so we can find a good solution for both of us."

3. Keep a Broad Focus: Look at the Big Picture

Another way to strengthen a weak position is to look at a larger time frame or a bigger scope.

Example: Your small manufacturing firm is negotiating with your sole supplier for an essential component in one of your biggest-selling products. Your supplier is a very large corporation. You represent a very small part of their business. They have just notified you of a substantial price increase of this essential component part. It would appear that you are in a very weak position. Here is an example of what you might say in an attempt to strengthen your position: "Troy, we are a young company, but have very strong management [describe it] and great growth potential. Although we represent a small percentage of your current business, we are confident we will become a major buyer in a few short years. Let me share our projected growth, and what this would mean to you in future business . . ." [Then provide well-documented projections.] Looking at this big picture could significantly strengthen your firm's position.

In any weak position situation, expanding the scope (broader focus, bigger picture, longer time frame) could strengthen your position. Here is another example: An employer is in a weak position because of the low starting salary they have to offer. They say to a job applicant, "That may be less than the salary you were looking for, but look at this chart and see how rapidly the average new hire increases their salary in the first two years with the organization. Don't overlook, also, the great benefits package, which starts immediately and is valued at . . ."

4. Seek a Better BATNA

BATNA is an acronym for one of the most important negotiation concepts: best alternative to negotiated agreement. In other words, what alternatives exist if an agreement is not reached with this party? For the first example we used in guideline 3 above, here are some suggestions for possible BATNAs:

- Could another supplier produce the critical part for you at a competitive price, perhaps with a minimum guaranteed annual volume?
- Could you produce this part?
- Could you use some other available part to accomplish the same purpose, even if it required some modification to the final product?

None of these may be great alternatives compared with buying the part at the existing price from the "sole supplier," but knowing your alternatives strengthens an otherwise weak position. The BATNA that you create doesn't even need to be better, *in your mind*, than the existing offer. The seller doesn't know whether it is or isn't better than their his proposal. *Remember, perception is reality.*

If it could possibly be an alternative, you may share it with the other party at the appropriate time. You might say: "Quite frankly, your price increase has put us in a real bind. We have to begin looking at other alternatives if you can't do any better on the price. Our projections show that your proposed price increase would take us out of the competitive market, and might just do us in. We'll have to begin exploring alternatives like . . . [name the alternatives you've identified]. I hope you will consider taking this back to your company to see if there isn't some way you could do better for us on the price. We sure have enjoyed our relationship with you the last three years." It's hard to be offended when it is stated in that manner. Creating alternatives, and then selecting the best one, can greatly strengthen an otherwise weak position.

5. Use a Team or Add an Expert

When appropriate, using a team (see chapter 10, "Team Negotiating") or adding an expert (see page 55) provides significant strength to a weak position. Advantages include:

- Strength in numbers
- Moral support
- Better planning
- More expertise
- Opportunities to play different roles (good guy/bad guy)
- Less chance for error

6. Find Needs

Nothing strengthens a weak position as much as knowing the unique needs of the other party. As mentioned in the introduction, two areas of needs are always present:

- The needs relating to the specific negotiation itself (what they want to accomplish in the negotiation)
- The needs of their personality style or type as it relates to the *process* of the negotiation

Knowledge of the second area of needs often separates the good from the great negotiators. Why? People are different but they are *predictably* different. Their personality style means they want to be treated in a unique way based on their likes and dislikes.

- Some like to move fast through negotiations; others prefer a slower pace.
- Some like to make decisions based on the facts; others, on how they "feel."
- Some like to be in control; others would rather follow.
- Some like to talk; others like to listen and ask questions.
- Some like to get to the task at hand; others prefer to build relationships.

By knowing the other party's personality needs, you can often accomplish what you want by satisfying their needs.

Example: I had the pleasure of serving as the convention chair for the National Speakers Association. With over fifty speakers needed to present various general sessions, breakout sessions, luncheons, and keynotes, it may come as a surprise that our speaker budget was zero. How can we attract speakers, many of whom are accustomed to earning $10,000 to $20,000 or more, to speak for free? The answer is simple. We find the unique needs they have and show them how this particular presentation can fill them. Of course, the needs are different for different people.

- Some celebrity speakers have a need to "give back" to the industry, and see this as a way of doing just that.
- Others speakers realize that most of the top speaker bureaus and agents in the country will attend the convention, and thus the speaker views it as a promotional opportunity.
- Still other speakers like to be quoted. If that's the case, we simply point out how the 1,500-plus speakers in attendance will be quoting them to millions of people over the next several years.

Knowledge of the other party and their needs in the negotiation may be the single most important factor for success when you are in a weak position.

One final suggestion: What is your thought process when you find yourself in a weak position? Here is what I do—I say, "Anybody can do well when they're in a strong position. This is going to be fun. I'll take everything I've learned about negotiating and turn my weak position into a strong position, or at least a moderate position." I like challenges. Some of you do also. It's all about attitude. Keep it positive and you'll do much better than if you dwell on your weak position.

6
Handling Difficult Negotiators

Let us never negotiate out of fear,
but let us never fear to negotiate.
—John F. Kennedy

Difficult people! We all encounter them sooner or later—the emotional, irrational, or illogical negotiators. These personality traits usually, but not always, emerge in situations filled with anxiety, tension, or unusually high stress levels. The other party could care less about "win-win" or "relationships." They just want the best deal they can get. Don't be frustrated when you find you have to negotiate with such a person. Keep your wits about you. Sometimes it's just a tactic they believe will have an adverse effect on you. They may simply be trying to rattle your cage. Don't play into their game. One or more of the following suggestions should help, and using them will separate you from the average negotiator.

1. Separate the People from the Problem
I often ask my audiences whether they should be a "hard" or a "soft" negotiator. I usually get a good number who

say "hard" and a good number who say "soft." Neither answer is exactly right. The best approach is to be both. You can be both hard and soft, if you carefully separate the *people* from the *problem*. Be hard (firm) on the problem; be soft (gentle) on the people.

What do I mean by this? As mentioned previously, you and the other party have two interests—the negotiation itself, and the relationship with the other party. It's true that a difficult negotiator may have no concern for their relationship with you. Generally, concessions can be made on the process of the negotiation—the environment, the timetable, and other procedural details—while holding firm on the important terms of the negotiation itself.

Apply firm negotiating strategies, tactics, and techniques to the problem; use partnering principles (see pages 5–16) with the other party.

Example: Here is a difficult situation where John was able to separate the people from the problem. He decided it was necessary for him to use one of the toughest of all strategies, the walkout (see page 172). This he used on the problem. However, on the other party, John used four of the partnering principles (PP) to soften his walkout strategy. Here is how he did it: "Phil, we've been good customers of yours for many years now, and I hope it will continue for many years in the future. [PP 1—Last Forever] Here is my situation. On this project, our board of directors said we must come in with a bid below $700,000 or we will simply not move forward with the project. Fortunately for us, we already have a bid under that figure. [PP 7—Open Communications] I understand how you feel [PP 4—Feelings as Facts], and hope you won't take offense. [PP 5—No Personal Offense] Do you have any thoughts on how we could make this a good deal for both of us?" John was tough on the problem, soft on the people.

2. Be Reflective

One of the most effective techniques with someone who is upset or unreasonable is to simply reflect back to them what you thought they said to you.

Example: "Let me see if I understand you, Julie. What I hear you saying is . . . [restate back to Julie what you thought you heard her say]." This does not necessarily mean that you agree with Julie, but only that you understand her feelings and thoughts. Take care not to parrot, because it could be perceived as patronizing. After hearing what you thought you heard her say, Julie will realize one of three things:

- That what she said was not logical, practical, and/or reasonable. Often people are so upset they don't even realize what they are saying. She may then retract or restate what she said.
- That she did not communicate well what she intended. She may then restate what she really meant, thus clearing up a major misunderstanding.
- That what she said was exactly what she meant to say. Ouch! Now you must go back to the drawing board and start asking questions that might help you both get on the same page (see chapter 1 on questions).

3. Give Positive, Nonverbal Feedback

When someone is upset, it's amazing what you can accomplish with the effective use of body language (see chapter 8). Help the other party feel comfortable. Lean forward, nod occasionally, and use reflective facial expressions. Decreasing your eye contact, crossing arms and/or legs, and a lack of facial expression could create increased tension or hostility. Honest, sincere motives toward the other party will typically bring about the appropriate nonverbal expressions. Make sure that your expressions are genuine!

4. Take Notes as a Technique

When people are upset or complaining, taking notes communicates interest and caring, and tends to reduce the other party's concerns. Taking notes can be used effectively on the telephone, saying something like, "Excuse me, could you slow down just a minute, I'm jotting down your concerns so I can be sure I understand the situation completely." What a difference! All of a sudden the person realizes you care, and hopefully the barriers go down.

5. Rarely Respond to a Hostile Remark with a Hostile Remark

Generally fight fire with water, not fire. Good negotiators have learned not to fall into the trap of responding in like manner to a hostile comment. One of the most effective approaches is to probe for the reason for the hostility, trying to get to the core of it. Allow the other party to keep venting, if necessary, until no hostility remains.

Notice the title of this section says "rarely." It does not say "never." In rare cases, it may be useful to respond aggressively. This rare case would typically need to meet all *four* of the following criteria:

- The other party is significantly off base in their position or opinion.
- It is a situation where you would be willing to walk away if it failed.
- If you aggressively confront the other party, in an attempt to change their mind, you would have a reasonable chance of success.
- You (or someone available to you) are the likely person who could accomplish this.

If you choose to respond forcefully, do it with full control of your emotions. This may be more difficult than you think (I recommend practicing with a teenager first). When one or both parties lose control of their emotions, rarely is anything positive accomplished. Valuable relationships are often permanently destroyed. If you feel physically threatened, exit the situation immediately.

6. When the Other Party Is Hostile or Feels Hurt, Express Sorrow and Empathy Without Accepting Responsibility

Example: "Tom, I'm so sorry you are in this situation. It must be very difficult for you." Often this reduces anxiety on the part of the other party. The expression and recognition of feelings are critical to successful negotiations. When you assist the other party to openly express their feelings, you often clear communication channels and improve the negotiating climate.

7. Rarely Issue an Ultimatum

An ultimatum usually backs you, or the other party, into a corner. It makes compromise and saving face for one or the other party more difficult. For example, you want to avoid asking questions or making statements like the following:

- "Is that your final offer?" When the other party says, "Yes," you have backed them into a corner. You have made it impossible for the other party to provide any more concessions, because you strongly encouraged them to say, "Yes, this is my final offer."
- "There is nothing else I can do [i.e., no other concessions can I make]." You have backed yourself into a corner; you can't make further concessions and still save face.

The skilled negotiator also knows how to help himself or the other party "save face" once backed into a corner. The key to this rescue mission is finding additional information (not available previously) that justifies a reexamination of the "final offer." For example:

- "Tara, I know you said that was your final offer, but here is some new information that may cause you to reconsider . . ."
- "Amy, I know I said there were no additional concessions I could make, but fortunately today the prime rate was lowered, giving us a few more options."

As in guideline 5 above, notice I say "rarely," rather than "never." There are certain situations where a "take it or leave it" strategy (see page 162) is more powerful, and worth the increased risk.

8. Eliminate the Words "But," "Fair," and "Reasonable" from Your Negotiating Vocabulary

The word "but" can always be replaced with the word "and" without changing the meaning of the sentence and still communicate your intent.

Example: "I like your proposal, *but* I'd like to suggest . . ." can more effectively be stated as, "I like your proposal *and* I'd like to suggest . . ." Using "and" is less offensive and much more positive than using "but."

The words "fair" and "reasonable" are emotion-filled words. Both can easily be replaced with the word "acceptable." It's certainly not that we don't want to be fair or reasonable; it's that what is fair or reasonable to one party might appear to be unfair and unreasonable to another party. What we really want to achieve is an agreement "acceptable" to both parties.

Example: Instead of saying, "Would it be fair if . . . ?" or "Would it be reasonable if . . . ?" say, "Would it be acceptable if . . . ?" This careful choice of words separates the good negotiator from the great negotiator.

In addition to the above techniques, I suggest reviewing the partnering principles discussed in the introduction. All of them may be helpful, but pay particular attention to:

- Recognize feelings as facts (page 10)
- Take no personal offense (page 11)
- Determine ahead of time how to resolve differences (page 15)

Not every difficult negotiator is going to change, but stranger things have happened. Remain positive. Applying these techniques just might surprise you. One other major point: these techniques, and those taught in other chapters, are principles that can and should be used a very high percentage (90 to 95 percent) of the time. Skilled negotiators realize, however, that some situations require action that would be exactly opposite of the stated principle. For instance:

- Sometimes it may be appropriate to give *negative* nonverbal feedback.
- Sometimes it may be appropriate to respond to a hostile remark *with a hostile remark*.
- Sometimes it may be appropriate to issue an *ultimatum*.

When would it be appropriate? That's what makes negotiation an "art" as well as a "science." The science you can learn by reading this book or attending a good seminar. The art you learn by applying the science (the principles) many times and then using your gut (educated intuition) to tell you when to ignore that principle. More about this in the conclusion.

7
Alternatives at an Impasse

Mutual consent is like a river.
which must have its banks on either side.
—Alain-René Lesage

Other chapters of this book build the pattern or mosaic to move smoothly through the negotiation process with knowledge, skill, and expertise. This chapter is different. Think of it as a first aid kit. It's not used in all negotiations. However, keep it close. When it is needed, it's very needed. It may be essential when a problem occurs. In negotiating, we call those problems impasses.

You've probably experienced it. You've come to the point in the negotiation when you say, "We're stuck! There is no way to continue! The negotiation is over!" More often than not, there are ways over, under, around, or through the obstacle. At least one of the parties needs to have an open mind to explore other possibilities.

Caution: When you reach an impasse, you are in dangerous territory. Using any one or more of these alternatives may not work. There is risk involved. You may be misunderstood. Challenging negotiations are not for the fainthearted. However, what is the alternative? End the negotiation? Great negotiators don't end a negotiation without exhausting all possibilities. Here are twenty-six possibilities, twenty-six creative alternatives when an impasse occurs. They are grouped into six general categories:

- Change Something in the Negotiation
- Rebuild Momentum
- Add Some Type of Bonus
- Tap Into the Feeling Side of Negotiating
- Use an Outside Party
- Try Time-Tested Techniques

Important: Before considering any of the alternatives, the big question to ask yourself (and sometimes the other party) is, "Why has it stalled?" If you can get at least some notion of the reason, you will have the foundational knowledge to decide which alternatives may overcome this impasse. It is not possible for me to tell you when to use each of these alternatives, although for some, I have suggested below when or where they could be best used. Usually, however, the decision on when to use an alternative depends on each unique situation. More often than not, at any given impasse many alternatives may be used before a solution is found. Don't hesitate to use one after another.

CHANGE SOMETHING IN THE NEGOTIATION

1. Change Locations
A change of scenery can often stimulate creativity. When you face an impasse, consider changing seating positions,

lighting, and table shapes and sizes. These small but important changes could overcome an impasse.

Examples:

- Move from the formal office setting to lunch at a nice restaurant.
- Move from a small room to a larger one or vice versa.
- Move from a room with formal chairs around a table to a room with comfortable couches and chairs.

2. Change the Shape of the Money

When money is involved in a negotiation (and it usually is), consider changing its shape when an impasse occurs. This could involve changing:

- The payment schedule
- The interest rates
- The amount of down payment
- Larger payments to smaller payments with a balloon payment at the end

Consider building variables or options into any of the suggested changes above. Creativity is the key here, combined with relative value. What can we change about the shape of the money that will provide a win for both parties?

Example: The buyer has a cash flow problem. The seller is trying to get the best return on their investments. The solution: lower down payment, longer terms, higher interest rates. Everyone wins!

3. Change Specifications

Rearranging the specifications or the terms of an agreement can often provide a creative alternative at an impasse. How could you change the terms of the agreement to provide mutual advantage? Be creative. Keep an open mind.

Example: Changing the shape of the widget slightly enables the manufacturer to use existing tooling, saving thousands and allowing them to reduce the cost for the buyer, while the manufacturer increases their profit margin. A true win-win.

Example: A newly hired employee works from 6:00 a.m. to 2:00 p.m., Monday through Friday. Her husband's only day off is Friday. She knows that Saturday and Sunday are the least desirable days for most people to work. She tells her boss that she would be happy to work Saturdays rather than Fridays. Her boss easily makes the change. Another true win-win.

Example: You have contracted to have your newly completed home landscaped. The completion date in the contract is the end of this month. Your landscaper calls to say the rock that you selected for a portion of the landscaping will not be in until the end of next month. They indicate they were hoping you would come in and select another type of rock because it would save them time and money to do the complete landscaping job at once, rather than putting in the rock later. You say you will talk with your husband and get back in touch with them. (Good for you! You don't make a quick decision. You and your husband will brainstorm together and get back with a plan.) Or, if no one else is involved, you let the landscaper know you will think about it and get back to them. The specifications changed; fortunately for you, they created an opportunity. You can get a better grade of rock (or an upgrade somewhere else on the landscaping) and, at the same time, help your landscaper save money. Be creative to work out a good deal for both of you.

4. Change the Negotiator or a Team Member

Obviously, adding a new personality to a negotiation can provide a fresh, new approach. It allows you, in essence, to start afresh in the negotiation. The selection of the individual inserted is highly important. What must be accomplished to overcome the impasse? Select the individual carefully, taking into account their behavioral style, their perceived expertise, and their credibility.

Example: In a major real estate transaction between two high-powered negotiating teams, Team A adds a city zoning expert to predict the probability of a future change in zoning which, if the zoning is changed, would greatly strengthen Team A's proposition.

Example: I was recently asked by a friend to advise her and her teenage child (with a mild learning disability) on how to persuade the school psychologist, social worker, and curriculum director that the student would be better off remaining in the regular high school system rather than being transferred to special education. I suggested that they add me to their team in the next discussion for three reasons: (1) my PhD provided a balance of credibility (see "Legitimacy Power," page 45) with the school psychologist, also a PhD, (2) adding me to their team made the numbers even (three vs. three), and (3) I could bring a fresh perspective. During the meeting, I said very little. My presence (1 and 2 above) seemed to make the difference. The negotiation concluded with a favorable result.

5. Change the Timetable

Time is absolutely critical in most negotiations (see "Time Power," page 58). How can you use it to one or both parties' advantage?

- Could you delay (or move up) the scheduled delivery or closing date?
- Could you extend the terms with agreeable interest rates applied?
- In a real estate transaction, could you as a seller allow the buyer to take possession a month earlier so the children can start school on time?

Examples:

- "Is there anything you can suggest that might help either one or both of us, from a time standpoint?"
- "Would you consider reducing the price if we were able to extend the delivery schedule?"
- "If we were willing to sign a two-year agreement rather than a one-year agreement, what additional considerations could you provide?"

Notice the open-ended nature of the last question. You might get much more than you expected. Besides, something like extending from a one- to a two-year contract might be just as desirable for your company.

6. Change Levels

Changing your negotiating position up or down a level can be an excellent alternative to an impasse. For the details of this alternative, see "Changing Levels," page 182.

REBUILD MOMENTUM

Negotiating is like an athletic contest—momentum is paramount. This can be done in at least three different ways:

7. Recap or Summarize

The process of negotiating is often a detailed and complex one. When an impasse occurs, it helps to go back and review the progress and the agreements made up to that point. It's often encouraging to note how much has already been accomplished . . . and it builds all-important momentum.

Example: "Well, let's see, Cynthia, we've already agreed on . . . [list all the agreed points]. The rest should be a walk in the park."

8. Introduce Another Issue

When an impasse is reached, one of the very best techniques can be to switch temporarily to another issue. Move to an issue on which you are likely to get a quick agreement. Again, it builds the momentum temporarily lost in the impasse.

Example: "Jaxon, it looks like we've reached an impasse on this issue. What would you think about moving to the next issue and see if we can solve that one? Then we can go back to this issue later." You will almost always get a positive response. If not . . . well . . . you have twenty-five other alternatives that may work.

9. Get an Agreement in Principle

Get agreement on anything you can get agreement on—even if it is only agreement in principle.

Example: You might agree that in the past you have always been able to come to a mutually agreeable solution: "Jay, in the three years that we have been working together, we've always been able to put together the deal, haven't we?"

Alternatively, you might agree on a mutual time deadline for completing negotiations: "Jay, let's say if we don't solve this problem by 5:30, we pick it up again tomorrow. Does that work for you?"

You might even agree on an objective procedure to resolve major differences, as shown in partnering principle 8 on page 15.

All these represent examples of getting agreement in principle to help rebuild the momentum of the negotiation.

ADD SOME TYPE OF BONUS

10. Suggest a Conditional Concession

When reaching an impasse, consider making a conditional concession. You would agree to concede one thing if they would concede another. As you consider making a conditional concession, remember the concept of relative value (page 77). Relative value simply means that individual items in a negotiation may have different values to the parties involved. If you can concede something with a relatively low value to you, that has a high value to the other side, then it's a mutually valuable concession. Obviously the reverse is also true.

Example: I was negotiating an office lease and had reached an impasse. I was not willing to pay the amount the landlord was asking. I offered to rent a larger suite of offices for a longer period of time, if he would make the price concession I wanted. The conditional concession worked. It was a great deal for both of us. The longer lease was obviously an advantage to him, but also to me because I wouldn't need to move again as long as we had room to expand as we grew. I could easily lease the extra offices to someone else initially, since we wouldn't need them in the beginning of the lease period. Additionally, I could control the length of the sublease, so I could plan my expansion without having to move offices—a true win-win situation.

11. Disclose Something

Making the decision to disclose confidential information is always difficult in a negotiation. Obviously, there are many reasons why certain confidential information should not be revealed. However, when you get to an impasse, the disclosure of some confidential information may lead to a win-win solution. This is particularly true when you feel the other party has demonstrated a true partnering approach and may be willing to share some confidential information with you.

Example: As a manufacturer, you would not normally share with your top distributor your costs to produce what they are buying from you. However, in this situation, they are threatening to move their business to one of your major competitors because they feel you are making an exorbitant profit. In this situation, you may choose to share some or all of the normally confidential manufacturing costs in hope of retaining their confidence in you and thus their business.

Your disclosures may also encourage similar disclosures from the other party, particularly when accompanied by a question such as, "Do I know everything I should know in regard to this matter?" When you ask that question, what is the other party thinking? They are probably thinking, "What have I not disclosed that I probably should have disclosed?" When the other party sees you as a partner, they are more likely to share (or trade) confidential information. This technique is more commonly used today than in the past because more people are using a partnering approach.

12. Use the Add-On Tactic

This alternative simply sweetens the deal by adding something of value when you reach an impasse. A wise negotiator often withholds something in order to offer it later for this very purpose, or they may seek to find some additional item that they may be able to offer, as in the following example:

"We are so close, Matthew. If we could reach agreement today, I might be able to get my manager to approve throwing in [name some extra thing]. What do you think?"

If he says yes, say, "You mean, if I can get him to throw in [the extra thing] at no additional cost, we've got a deal?" If Matthew responds affirmatively, say, "All right, I'll give it a try." This leaves Matthew hoping you can get it approved, rather than developing cold feet and wondering if he should have ever committed to the deal.

If he says no, say, "That's okay. I don't think I would have been able to get my manager to approve that anyway." Notice how that statement levels the playing field. The implication is that your suggested compromise would not have been accepted anyway.

13. Provide a Guarantee

This technique is particularly effective when the other party perceives the risk of the transaction to be greater than you believe it to be. Sometimes a party is reluctant to agree not because of the particular terms of the agreement, but because they are concerned that certain terms of the agreement may not be fulfilled. Simply eliminate the risk by providing a guarantee.

Example: This principle really worked well in the marketing of my educational products. Some clients would look at the price and ask, "How do I know it will be worth the price?" I quickly realized I could eliminate any concerns by providing a money-back guarantee—if they didn't get at least three times the ROI (return on investment) they could simply send it back in the first year for a complete refund. Sales increased immediately. I had eliminated the buyer's risk.

Other examples:

- Automobile dealerships provide warranties on new and used vehicles, knowing that the increased number of vehicles they sell more than adequately pays for the cost of repairs.
- Retailers offer a "lowest price guarantee" to build legitimacy that their prices are the lowest (and rarely have to provide a refund or a lower price).
- The seller of a home guarantees the buyer that they will cover the cost of reroofing the house if it leaks within the first year. The seller is confident the roof will last at least several years. The guarantee seals the transaction and is worth the risk.
- A handyman guarantees that his services will be acceptable to the homeowners or they don't pay him.
- The employee requests a "no transfer" guarantee in their employment contract so that they are assured they and their family can be permanently located in the area.

14. Add Options

What option could be added to the transaction that could be a plus for one or both parties? Even if it is an advantage to only one party, it may enable the parties to put together an otherwise difficult agreement. Creativity is the key here.

Example: The agent for an outstanding rookie quarterback was negotiating a proposed three-year contract with a National Football League team. It was the day before training camp was to begin. Both the team and the agent hoped to have the QB in camp the next day but they were hundreds of thousands of dollars apart. The team representative asked the agent, "Why is this QB worth what you are asking?"

After a brief pause, the agent said, "Because of his playing time over the next three years of this contract . . . " and the agent listed the playing time he felt confident the quarterback would get in each of those three years.

The team asked for a brief recess. Rather quickly they returned with a new proposal—the base salary that the team had previously offered, plus a bonus (option) based on the QB's playing time each year, which totaled exactly what the agent was looking for. How could he refuse? The perfect use of an option to overcome an impasse. The rookie had a signed contract that day and was in training camp the next morning. They bridged a several-hundred-thousand-dollar gap in less than an hour with the creative use of an option.

TAP INTO THE FEELING SIDE OF NEGOTIATING

15. Recognize and Express Feelings

This is a great technique used by those who understand the importance emotion plays in a transaction. (For further insight, see "Recognize Feelings as Facts," on page 10.) Both parties expressing feelings can often clear the air for further progress. Remember you don't have to *agree with* or *endorse* the other party's feelings. Just recognizing them can go a long way in making the other party feel more comfortable.

Example: "Hunter, I sure feel frustrated and discouraged that we haven't reached an agreement yet. What are your feelings right now?"

Continue to share feelings, as appropriate, expressing your feelings and trying to draw out feelings from the other party. Remember our discussion of "Feelings First, Then Think!" It is hard to think clearly when you don't understand or recognize your own feelings. It's hard to know the other party's needs when you don't know what they are feeling. Often a part of their need is for them to know that you understand their feelings.

16. Use Empathy

The use of empathy is particularly effective with open, relationship-oriented personalities. Expressing empathy, particularly to this kind of individual, strengthens relationships and stimulates a partnering environment.

Example: "Mark, I think I know what it is like in your position. Just last month I was in this type of situation myself when . . ." Using empathy may also be combined effectively with the feel, felt, found strategy (page 185).

17. Use Humor

Properly applied humor can go a long way in releasing tension and loosening a tight situation at an impasse.

Example: In a recent negotiation one team indicated a 5:00 p.m. deadline was needed in their behalf. As the deadline was about to be reached, the other team said they assumed that was Pacific Standard Time since they were all from California and had just flown into Chicago for the meeting. They all had a good laugh at the confusion, loosening up a tension-filled meeting, and providing an extra two hours of negotiating time.

USE AN OUTSIDE PARTY

18. Bring In an Expert

This alternative uses expert power (see page 55) in an attempt to overcome an impasse. The added power and legitimacy that an expert can provide often gives the slight edge in a difficult negotiation. In addition to their new ideas and their credibility, an expert often supplies additional momentum.

Examples:

- An attorney for legal expertise
- A CPA for accounting expertise
- An engineer or scientist for technical expertise
- An MD for medical expertise
- J. D. Power and Associates for an industry-wide perspective
- A negotiation expert for that big deal

19. Refer to a Joint Study Committee

In major negotiations, one alternative when an impasse occurs is to refer the matter to a joint study committee, which may provide additional ideas and options. This committee could be made up of representatives from each organization engaged in this negotiation. The use of nonnegotiating personnel in this regard, who can explore all possibilities with an open mind, often creates win-win solutions reached in no other way. The joint study committee simply makes their findings known to the actual negotiators from each side, hopefully providing some new ways to look at the problems.

Example: Two trade associations in closely related industries, although direct competitors in many respects, have several opportunities to promote similar causes. The two executive directors (paid leaders of each association) negotiate with each other in an attempt to build a coalition that can meet their mutual needs. Things are not progressing well, so one group's president (an elected member who is not paid) approaches his counterpart in the other group, suggesting that they each select four people from their respective associations to form an eight-member joint study committee. The committee will meet and submit suggestions to both presidents and both executive directors, who will then decide if and what further action might be taken.

20. Use a Mediator or Arbitrator

Getting a third party involved is often a great option at an impasse, particularly when the stakes are high for both parties. Agreeing ahead of time, or even when stalled, to put some or all of the decision-making power in the hands of a third party (like a mediator or an arbitrator) can be a wise decision. This is particularly true when not reaching an agreement is a disaster for both parties. Many work stoppages and strikes fall into this category. You might suggest this to the other party by saying, "Rob, this is really a big deal for both of us.

Somehow, we've got to reach an agreement. I've been thinking about ways that we might do that reasonably for both us. What about using a neutral third party?"

A mediator tries to bring the respective sides to agreement, whereas an arbitrator generally has the power to make decisions should the parties not reach agreement on their own. A great technique to bring parties closer together is for an arbitrator to ask both sides to bring their suggestion for the most reasonable settlement. The arbitrator then chooses one or the other party's *most reasonable settlement offer.* Obviously, this eliminates highballing or lowballing (page 175). Often both parties submit offers close to each other, realizing the arbitrator is going to select the *most reasonable* one.

21. Appeal to an Ally

Who can be your ally? Is there anyone who can influence the other party, such as a mutual friend, business associate, family member, or someone else close to the other party? Could they directly or indirectly influence that person? If so, appeal to that ally for help.

Example: "Emma, might I suggest you talk to Jan Hill. She has used us for more than two years and has been extremely pleased with the results." Or you might have Jan give Emma a call, if appropriate.

In team negotiations, look to the other negotiating team for an ally. Is there someone that seems easiest to work with or most open to compromise? If so, direct your negotiations to that individual. In other words, seek the path of least resistance through the opposing team. Build allies.

TRY TIME-TESTED TECHNIQUES

22. Take a Recess

Sometimes something as simple as taking a break can help you relax, release tension, and cause the creative juices to flow. It is true that the problem may not go away, but the way you approach the impasse may change. Mind-sets, both yours and the other party's, may change with the passage of time, and this may be just what is needed to break the deadlock. The length of the break should be appropriate to the circumstance, but within reason; the longer the better—even to the extent of postponing for a day or longer. Spend at least a portion of the break relaxing. Then say to yourself, "How can I look at this in a different way?" Talk to family members, friends, and associates for advice.

Example: "Margaret, I've got an idea. Why don't we take a break and resume our discussion this afternoon— what does your schedule look like?"

Four out of five times the other party will agree to the break. As you break, encourage the other party to do just what you plan on doing—relaxing and trying to look at things from a different perspective.

23. Use Doomsday Tactics

Although this tactic focuses on negative rather than positive, explaining the dire consequences of not reaching an agreement can sometimes shock the other party into a concession or an agreement. In using this tactic to overcome an impasse, consider how it might be presented in a positive way. It may be your sincere concern for the other party that will cause you to point out their dire consequences. Even when discussing negatives, you can often do it in a way that builds, rather than destroys, relationships.

Example: A union/management dispute is about to cause a work stoppage. When both parties look at the dire consequences for each, it's a very gloomy picture indeed. If an agreement is not reached, both parties will suffer greatly. That "doomsday" condition should motivate each party to seek arbitration or mediation. "Coreen, I've analyzed this situation from every angle I can. Our organizations will both be in rough shape if you and I can't get this resolved. Where might we mutually concede to reach an agreement?"

Example: You are attempting to buy the home of someone who is facing foreclosure. You explain to them their two options: (1) they can sell the home to you even if they don't get quite what they want for it, or (2) they can let it go into foreclosure, get no cash at all, and greatly damage their reputation and credit rating. The first scenario is not good, but the second is a real disaster.

24. Present a Hypothetical Situation

Hypothetical questions will often stimulate creative thinking in the other party. You can use them to shift their thinking in a direction more favorable to your position or proposal by helping them see situations and circumstances they have not considered before.

- "What would happen if I were able to get my wife to agree that you could take possession of the home March 1?"
- "If we moved the completion date earlier by two months, would that be an advantage to you?"
- "I could get you no-interest financing for a year, with no payments until November. Would that work for you?"

Note that in the first question, possession of the home is not being offered on March 1, but rather there is the chance that it may be, if *the wife* would agree. In the other two questions, it appears that these hypothetical situations can be made a reality with an affirmative answer from *the other party*. In presenting hypothetical situations, it is normally better to pose the question like the first one—in a way that an affirmative answer means that the other party would favorably conclude the agreement providing you are able to get approval (which you may or may not get). That way the power stays on your side, in that the other party has agreed to move ahead if you can get approval.

25. Illustrate

The creative use of a flip chart, a whiteboard, a PowerPoint presentation, or simply putting it on paper so all parties can see your (and, in some cases, the other party's) point of view is often an alternative that provides the slight edge in overcoming an impasse. Reducing facts and figures, agreements and disagreements, to writing provides clarification, often making an impasse easier to overcome.

Example: I was once hired to consult with a professional golfer who wasn't reaching his full potential on the tour. I asked him to reduce to writing where he wanted to be one, five, and twenty years from now. After having great difficulty with this for several weeks, and with a lot of prodding on my part, he finally completed the assignment. His comment was, "This really helped. Once I had it on paper, I could see what I needed to do and when I needed to do it." He was back on track. His golf game improved greatly. Writing crystallizes thought, and crystallized thought motivates action. Both crystallized thought and motivated action are often necessary in overcoming an impasse.

Example: One party in a negotiation suggests, "We are at an impasse and there are four items on which we disagree. Together, let's list these four items and make a copy for each of us. Then you and I will both briefly summarize on that sheet our positions on these four items and give the other person a copy." It has been my observation that when this occurs, both parties are able to suggest ideas that may solve their impasse. Party A might suggest that if Party B could make a certain concession on item 1, Party A could make a different concession on item 3. Party B might suggest that if Party A could make a certain concession on item 2, Party B could make a concession on item 4. It's amazing the clarity that can occur when differences are reduced to writing.

26. Postpone

When all else fails, don't assume that the negotiation is over. In many cases, you can postpone the negotiation, indefinitely if necessary, rather than terminating it. This alternative is effectively used when (1) the passage of time itself may provide a solution, and (2) when nothing else seems to have worked. It's the court of last appeal, so to speak.

Well, there you have it—your negotiating first-aid kit— the twenty-six "fixes" that may help when you are slowed or stopped in a negotiation. Sometimes you should use them in combination with each other. If one is not successful, move on to others. Some of them may have unfavorable side effects. Some of them require risk. Before using, be sure the potential side effects are worth the risk.

Keep this list handy. Many of my seminar partici- pants have reported to me months and even years later how these twenty-six alternatives have helped them over, under, around, or through a difficult impasse. I hope they will do the same for you.

PART 3

Adjust to Your Environment

What and where are you?

8
Body Language

As a rule, anything that is either shouted or whispered isn't worth listening to.
—Frederick Langbridge

The ability to read body language can be an invaluable asset in any interaction, particularly in a negotiation. People tend to have opposite opinions about the value of reading body language. They either discount it completely or tend to make too many decisions based on it. The truth is that we need to find a middle ground, where we realize that body language is an art, not a science. It's a tool that, with a little practice and study, can provide valuable insights into the feelings and thought processes of the other party.

Reading body language definitely is not an exact discipline. We can never know for certain that anyone who crosses his arms is defensive, or that anyone that puts her hand to her mouth is lying or unsure of herself, but body language can typically provide valuable insight about a person's emotional state. That having been said, you probably read body language better than you think you do. I often prove this to my audiences by projecting images of people in various types of interactions and asking what they think is happening. It is amazing the consistency and accuracy of their responses, even in other countries.

There are many cross-cultural consistencies in reading body language. However, there are also numerous and critical differences. An entire book could be devoted to cross-cultural similarities and differences in body language. Because of the scope of this topic, I will not attempt to discuss it here. I have mentioned previously the availability of CultureGrams for useful information on many cultures (see page 41).

There are three important reasons to study body language:

- *To observe what the other party may be feeling and thinking.* Studies have indicated that it is difficult to fake body language. A person skilled in reading it can gain valuable insight into the other party. It could be the opposite of what that other party is verbalizing.
- *To communicate more effectively.* Communication consists of three factors—the words you say, how you say them, and what you are doing with your body when you say them. I believe the last two to be at least as important as the words you choose.
- *To understand how your body language influences your own thinking and feeling.* We tend to think and feel in harmony with our body position. For example, if you are beginning an important negotiation and feel unsure of yourself, take a more confident body position. As the old song "I Whistle a Happy Tune,"

from *The King and I*, says, "Make believe you're brave / And the trick will take you far. / You may be as brave / As you make believe you are."

Now let's examine some generally accepted meanings of certain gestures and positions. One of the best ways to study body language is to examine confidence and nonconfidence gestures.

Confidence Gestures or Positions

• *The steeple* is a subtle, yet important, confidence gesture, the touching of the fingertips of one hand to the fingertips of the other hand. Generally, the higher the steeple is displayed, the greater the confidence. However, even a very subdued or reserved steeple can display a great deal of confidence. Look for it and be aware of it. I hate to be on the other side of the table from someone who is displaying a steeple. They may be saying, "I know something you don't know."

• *Hands behind the head, leaning back in the chair.* Visualize two attorneys, sitting with their hands clasped behind their heads, leaning back in their chairs. It is a sure sign of confidence because opening the body completely up usually means you don't feel vulnerable.

• *Thumbs displayed.* Visualize a man with his hand on the upper lapel of his suit jacket with his thumb exposed. Does he feel confident? No question about it.

Visualize a woman with both hands in the front or rear pockets of her jeans, again with her thumbs displayed. She is very confident and self-assured.

• *Possession gestures.* Picture the person with their hand, arm, or leg resting on an object such as a car, boat, building, desk, or even another person. You can just see them saying, "I own this and I feel confident about it."

• *Straddling position on a chair.* There are two things you can say about this individual. First, he is probably a very creative thinker and is expressing that creativity in the unique way he uses the chair. Second, he is definitely displaying confidence. That's not the position you'd take to talk to your new boss about a raise, particularly if you wanted to display the appropriate respect and humility.

• *Sustained eye contact* is another display of confidence. Keep in mind, of course, differences between people and differences between cultures. Some people and some cultures naturally maintain eye contact on a more consistent basis. As with any body language analysis, read it in a global context.

• *Hands clasped behind the back* is another good example of a confidant body position. Do you remember your high school principal or your commanding officer? Wasn't it customary for them to address your group with their hands clasped behind their back and perhaps with their head tilted back a bit, maybe even looking down their nose at you? Like all body positions and gestures, this may show someone who is feeling confident or it might be showing someone who is trying to make you think they feel confident. Body language is difficult, but not impossible, to fake. The more you study it, the better you read it, and the more likely you are to recognize a deceptive body position or gesture.

Nonconfident Gestures or Positions

- *The fig leaf.* I often demonstrate this one by selecting a male volunteer from my audience. I escort him to the front of the room and have him stand on an elevated platform. Then I step off to the side. The room becomes completely silent with all eyes on my volunteer. How is he standing? You guessed it—hands clasped in front of him in the typical fig-leaf position. He feels uncomfortable, exposed, and lacks confidence, and his body language reveals it.

- *Hand to the mouth or nose area.* Chances are the person is feeling nonconfident, doubting, or not sure of something. Probe for what that means by asking appropriate questions. Trained interrogators know that when most people tell a lie, they raise their hand to their nose or their mouth. It's important to point out that just because a person puts their hand to their mouth or nose, it does not necessarily mean they are lying or they lack confidence. They might simply have an itch on their nose. Always put body language into context.

• *Lack of eye contact* (or less eye contact than is normal for this person) is another sign of nonconfidence. This is a clue that you need to find out the source of the discomfort. Do they lack confidence in:

- What you are saying?
- What they are saying?
- Their ability to handle this negotiation?
- Your integrity?
- Their integrity?

• *Eye blink rate* as it compares to their normal blink rate. The faster the eye blink rate, the more the person is uncomfortable. Try this experiment; turn on a newscast and click "mute." Watch the eye blink rate of the newscaster. When they are reporting on a story with which they feel uncomfortable, their eye blink rate will increase. Experts teach customs agents to ask questions and then monitor eye blink. If it increases, they interrogate much more thoroughly.

Example: I was having an intense but friendly conversation with an acquaintance on a topic I felt strongly positive about. When I was through, he made an interesting comment: "Jim, you didn't blink your eyes once through that entire conversation!" Of course, I didn't realize it at the time, but I thought, "Wow, I really believed and wanted to communicate those important ideas to that person and I felt very positive about what I was saying." It showed in my eyes.

In relation to the three reasons for studying body language stated on page 122, use your knowledge of the confident and nonconfident gestures to:

- Know whether the other party feels confident or nonconfident by observing these gestures or body positions in them
- Communicate more effectively with the other party by using the confident or nonconfident gestures yourself, depending on how you want to appear
- Take these positions while in a negotiation or preparing for one, to help you feel more confident / nonconfident

You might ask, "Why would I want to appear or feel nonconfident?" The answer is that you can sometimes appear or feel overconfident, and this might be a "turn-off" to the other party.

Similarly use the gestures and positions listed below:

More Body Language Cues

- *The palms: open vs. closed.* An open palm indicates warmth, friendliness, openness, honesty, and submissiveness. Think of all the gestures that display open palms. Can you feel the warmth displayed by those open palms? The opposite is true with the closed palm or closed fist. Imagine the finger pointed downward, fist closed, and perhaps even pounding emphatically, while a forceful point is made. The closed palm represents force, power, control, and authority.

Even the handshake demonstrates this. Have you ever shaken hands with a person who, in addition to having a very firm handshake, had his palm facing down? The dominant person's hand comes over the top so his palm is down, in the power position, causing your palm to be in the up, or submissive, position. This may be a clue that someone wants to dominate or control.

• *Hand to the back of the neck.* Particularly if the person is rubbing the neck as if there is pain there, this is often a sign of annoyance, or a "pain in the neck." What the pain is, you determine by context and by skillful questioning.

• *Scratching the head.* Especially when it's accompanied with puzzling facial gestures, this tends to say, "This is not making sense." Ask questions. Find out what's not making sense.

• *A finger under the collar* normally indicates, "I'm hot under the collar," or "I'm upset or uncomfortable about something."

• *Eye pupil dilation.* This is a natural reaction, beyond our control, that occurs when we feel happiness, elation, or other positive feelings. The reverse is also true. There is a constriction of pupils when the person feels angry, upset, or in other ways agitated. If you are close enough to see the size of their pupils, you can read changes in them and infer what they may be feeling.

Example: Serious poker players sometimes wear dark glasses so that the natural reaction of their pupils dilating or constricting won't give them away. They can maintain a "poker face" regardless of the hand they are dealt.

• *Tilting the head* means a person is paying attention and that the message they are hearing is very important to them.

Example: You see this natural reaction in dogs. Visualize the master talking to his dog. Can't you just see the dog tilting its head as it listens intently to its master? People often do the same thing. Many times a person may appear to give you full attention, but you can be sure of it if they tilt their head.

• *Stroking the chin* usually means a person is curious, puzzled, has a possible sincere interest, is trying to decide, or has a desire to learn more. If you see someone doing this in a negotiation, give the person more information.

• *Hand supports the head.* Boredom or tiredness.

• *Feet and/or body orientation.* People tend to turn their body, and particularly their feet, toward the door or exit when they are thinking about or wanting to move in that direction.

• *A tug at the ear* usually means that the individual wants to hear more. Give them more information on what you are discussing.

• *An elevated position.* Sitting in a higher chair or standing when the other person is sitting gives a person a position of power—the more elevated, the more power. If you want to appear more powerful, seek an elevated position. If you want to appear friendly, humble, non-threatening, and approachable, position yourself at or below the other person's level. As a speaker, I like to meet as many people as I can before my presentations. If they are already seated and I'm standing, I'll often kneel down to be slightly below their level. It builds rapport and makes them feel comfortable. They might even think I'm a nice guy!

• *Mirroring* is taking the same body position as the other party, in an attempt to "get on the same wavelength" with them. If they are leaning back in their chair, you lean back in your chair. If they cross their arms and/or legs, you cross your arms and/or legs. Obviously, don't do it so simultaneously that the other party becomes aware of what you are doing. If you use this technique with care and caution, it does work.

• *Putting an object in the mouth*—such as a pen or eyeglasses—often means a person needs nourishment. Feed them more of what you are telling them. It is generally a positive sign in a negotiation. However, put the gesture into context. Like other gestures and body positions, it may simply be a habit (or they are ready for lunch!). Pay particular attention when the gesture is used infrequently (not like a habit). It's more likely to mean something in that situation.

• *Lint picking.* When the person with whom you are communicating is picking imaginary pieces of lint off their clothes, they are bored or have lost interest. Do something quickly to reignite their interest.

• *Folded arms and/or legs* normally implies a defensive position:

- "I'm not accepting what you are saying."
- "My mind is closed."

However, read this gesture in the context of other things. It may simply be that the other party is cold, or is comfortable in that position.

As I address my audiences, I notice that at any given time, 10 to 20 percent of participants have their arms folded. If a significantly larger percentage of the people have their arms folded, I'm probably in trouble. What does a good speaker or negotiator do in that situation? Remember the third reason we study body language: it influences our thinking. The longer the other party or the audience stays in that defensive position, the more likely they are to think negatively. A good negotiator says something to get the other party out of the negative position. It might be as simple as, "Could you please hand me that notepad?" or, "Of these three samples, point to the one you like best," or "Why don't we all stand for a moment to get the kinks out?" Pose any other question or statement that requires them to unfold their arms.

OTHER EXTERNAL CONSIDERATIONS

Room Layout

The physical surroundings can play an important part in any negotiation. Here are some factors to consider. Let's assume you are in your office so you are in control of the environment. The most powerful position for you is behind your desk (or table) with the other person's chair as far back from your desk as possible. Not a very cordial environment—but it does put you in the power position. That's not exactly my recommended style! I don't believe in negotiation by intimidation.

The closer the other party's chair is to you and/or your desk or table, the more you lose power and authority. You can create an even friendlier environment by moving the chair to the side of the desk where only a small portion of the desk remains between you and the other person. The most friendly, relaxed, and comfortable position for the other party would be for you to move out from behind your desk to one of the chairs in front so that you and the other party are in similar chairs and nothing at all separates the two of you.

Here is a question I often pose in my training seminar. Suppose you walk into a room to negotiate with someone who has already taken a position at the rectan-

gular table on a long side near one of the ends. Fortunately for you, there are three other chairs around the
table. You may choose your chair. Chair A is immediately beside the other party on the long side of the table.
Chair B is at the end of the table closest to that individual in a kitty-corner fashion. Chair C is opposite the individual and directly across the table. Wanting to be the
most effective in this negotiation, which of these chairs
would you choose?

The audience normally shouts, "A," "B," and "C" simultaneously. I agree with each choice, *depending upon
what they want to accomplish*. Those who said chair A,
the chair immediately alongside the person, were
thinking they wanted to create a friendly, comfortable,
relationship-building environment with no obstacles
between parties. Chair B, at the end of the table, affords flexibility (you can slide one way or the other)
and get some of the advantages of both positions A and
C. Additionally you have the advantage of being in the
power position at the head of a rectangular table. Others said chair C, the chair opposite the individual. That
would be the best selection if you wanted a more formal setting or if you had the power and wanted to
maintain it.

Dress and Color
Generally speaking, you project more power and authority when you dress slightly more formally than the
individual with whom you are negotiating. The color of
your clothing will often make a strong impression on

the other party. Dark blue is the single most effective color to project power. This is true for both men and women. Accessories that provide the most contrast, perhaps a white shirt or blouse and a red tie or accessory, would provide a strong impression of power. A light blue shirt or blouse, as an example, would not project nearly the power that the white shirt or blouse would. The brighter tie for a man, and brighter accessories for a woman, as long as they are fashionable, will also accentuate the power. It goes without saying that being in the latest style (without being overly trendy) is also important.

There are circumstances, even in a negotiation, where you do not want to project power. It might be to your advantage, in fact, to project just the opposite. When you think you might intimidate the other party, and that intimidation would not work to your advantage, choose nonpower colors. In order to project warmth and friendliness, wear warm earth tones without a great deal of contrast. You'd be amazed how important color is in projecting image and power.

I encourage you to study body language in situations where you are not under the pressure of negotiating. You may want to mute the TV and see how much you can understand by concentrating only on body language. Another excellent opportunity to study and learn body language is when you can observe a negotiation while not participating in it. I have even noticed a network news program that regularly invites a body language expert to evaluate political candidates and well-known leaders for their viewing audience. This is another excellent way to learn.

I have not attempted to give a complete course on body language in this book, but rather to stimulate your thinking and to give you a few tips that might be helpful in your next negotiation.

9
Telephone Negotiating

There is very little difference between people,
but the little difference makes a big difference.
—W. Clement Stone

The techniques shared, and concepts presented, in all chapters of this book (including the introduction and conclusion) apply equally well to telephone negotiating as they do in face-to-face negotiating. The purpose of this chapter is to point out the unique characteristics of telephone negotiation and the techniques and concepts that will give you the slight edge when using the telephone.

One's choice of words is very important on the phone, as this example demonstrates. If, when you call to speak to someone, her receptionist says, *"May I ask who's calling?"* it certainly sounds like she is screening calls. However, if the receptionist says, *"May I tell her who's calling?"* it sounds so much better and doesn't sound like screening (even though it may be!).

To use, or not to use, the telephone is an important decision in any negotiation. There is no simple, all-inclusive answer to that question. There are at least five distinct characteristics of telephone communication. Consider each when determining whether to use, or not use, the telephone in a negotiation.

• *It is quicker.* Obviously, telephone negotiations save time and money. This factor alone causes us to use the telephone in situations where the magnitude of the transaction does not justify the time and expense to get face-to-face. The telephone is a great place to start gathering information for any negotiation. You can ask many questions over the phone to better prepare you for negotiating in person later.

• *It leaves more room for misunderstanding.* Because it affords no opportunity to read body language—a major advantage in face-to-face communications—more misunderstandings can, and usually do, occur on the telephone. Make an extra effort to be clear on the telephone. Take the initiative to ask questions when there might be a misunderstanding. Take notes of the discussions and e-mail or send them to the other party to confirm the points you discussed—you would rather have it in writing the way *you* understood it.

• *Saying no is easier.* The telephone enables either party to say no more easily. If you fear a no or find yourself in a weak position, you may want to seek a face-to-face negotiation.

• *The advantage goes to the caller.* Other things being equal, the caller has the advantage because the caller is (or at least should be!) prepared. More mistakes are made in phone negotiations for this reason than any other. If you are the unprepared "callee," don't make the mistake of continuing in your unprepared state. Do whatever is necessary to exit the conversation until you are prepared. Come up with a logical reason why you cannot talk right then, and set up a time for a return call. Be alert for situations when you may be an unprepared callee, like when you receive a call:

- About an ongoing negotiation and you don't have your file with the important details at hand
- When you are about to enter an important meeting and cannot devote your full attention to this situation
- Asking for a decision that requires great thought and planning on your part

• *Using the phone eliminates "home field" advantage. Where* a negotiation takes place can have a critical effect on its outcome. If the other party has control of the environment and knows how to use it to their advantage (see chapter 8, "Body Language"), you may want to neutralize that advantage by negotiating by phone or in some other neutral place.

TELEPHONE NEGOTIATING TIPS

With the above characteristics in mind, let's look at what we can do to be particularly effective on the telephone.

1. Be Prepared

Of course, this is true for any negotiation, but it becomes even more important on the telephone. In addition to taking all the steps you would take in the normal face-to-face negotiation, be sure to have all available information and resources at your fingertips for the telephone negotiation.

- Would a computer and Internet access be helpful?
- Is a calculator necessary?
- Are there experts you may want to access by a conference call?
- Is there any other information you need at your fingertips, such as correspondence, reports, files, and so forth?
- Is there a list of questions you want to ask?
- Do you have an agenda that includes the points you want to emphasize?
- Would a speakerphone or cordless headset help?

If you are unprepared for any reason, exit. Do not feel you must negotiate just because someone has reached you by phone. Use whatever technique you feel comfortable with to postpone the negotiation until you are prepared.

Example:

"Excuse me, Tiana. Can I put you on hold for a moment?"

Place the party on hold for a few seconds and then say, "May I call you back in fifteen minutes? What does your schedule look like then?"

Nine times out of ten, they will agree, allowing you time to get prepared.

2. Take Notes

In a face-to-face negotiation, the importance of both eye contact and body language may dictate, at least in some situations, that you refrain from taking notes. However, always take notes on the telephone.

Example:

When one party says, "Christian, I see by my notes of our phone conversation on November 17, you said . . . ," it gives them knowledge power, legitimacy power, expert power (they're obviously an expert at what they do), and even commitment power—they're committed enough to this interaction to take notes. Be the party with the facts and figures. Use them to your advantage.

3. Use the Pause Effectively

The pause is particularly effective on the telephone. Although I mentioned this tip previously (see "Silence," page 33), it was specifically used for a different purpose. Here it has four other distinct purposes:

- *For emphasis.* Using a longer than normal pause emphasizes the key point(s) you want to address. The listener will take notice when they have a moment to reflect during your pause.
- *To help you get more information.* Have you noticed what happens when you pause in a telephone conversation? The other party starts to talk. More often than not, they give you valuable information that you would not have received otherwise.

- *To put pressure on the other party.* They do not know what you are thinking. They don't know why you are not speaking.
- *To say, "I feel comfortable in this situation."* It demonstrates confidence.

Effective use of the pause is the sign of a great negotiator.

4. Use Body Language

Use your knowledge of body language (from chapter 8) to project what you want to project. For instance, if you want to project power, try standing as you talk. Make other positive, confident body gestures. If, on the other hand, you want to project a warm, comfortable, friendly attitude, you might select a reclining chair and put your feet up in a relaxed position. Also use different tones of voice to project power or warmth.

Example: I had an office manager with one of the friendliest and cordial telephone voices I had ever heard. When I asked her about it, she said she had learned early in her career to put a big smile on her face before she answered (or called) on the telephone. It works! Body language can help you become more effective in communicating, even on the telephone.

5. Reduce Agreements to Writing

In addition to taking notes, whenever you agree on anything of substance on the phone, confirm it with a memo, letter, e-mail, fax, or text message. Experienced negotiators know the value of having agreements in writing. Who should reduce it to writing? *You should!* If there were a misunderstanding, you would much prefer to have it in writing the way you understood it.

The faintest ink is better than the fondest memory.

Example: I had agreed to do a series of public seminars sponsored by a promoter friend of mine. A year later at the break in the first seminar, he handed me a check that was $500 less than I thought we had agreed to a year before. He said, "No, this was the financial arrangement I remember agreeing to!" Because we were such good friends, we had not used the normal written agreement. I thought, "Have I followed my own advice—did I reduce it to writing?" I quickly went to my room to check my file. There it was—a copy of the memo I had sent him confirming the agreement—the way I had remembered it. He quickly agreed when he saw the memo. Confirming our verbal agreement in writing saved me thousands of dollars (and, perhaps, a broken friendship).

6. Use a Checklist or Partial Script

Although we don't want to sound scripted or formal on the phone, this doesn't mean we can't use an outline or even a partial script. When you have a particularly important negotiation, or when the same type of negotiation occurs often, a checklist or script can be very helpful in remembering the many important details. Asking the right questions in the right way, and having your key points well articulated, may give you the slight edge that tips the negotiation in your favor. When you have the need for a script, role-play the conversation, noting on paper the questions and points you want to make in the phone call. Having them organized and clearly visible in front of you, with a place to take notes, will make you more effective in your next telephone negotiation.

7. Avoid Distractions

I must confess I've made this mistake more times than I care to admit.

Example: You're at the airport. They're about to call your flight. You get a message that your business prospect wants to talk to you about closing that big deal, so you call back. The gate area is loud. It's crowded. You finally get the other party on the phone. The other party changes the offer considerably, but it's hard to tell whether it's better or worse for you. You are disoriented and not sure. Definitely the wrong time to make an important decision!

You can't concentrate in that environment and you shouldn't have put yourself in it. Get out of it any way you can. Wait until you can get somewhere you can concentrate and not be distracted. Take it from someone who has learned from several bad experiences—avoid making hurried, distracted decisions when negotiating by phone.

8. Use Telephone Technology to Your Advantage

What would we do without cell phones? They are not only convenient time-savers, but they contain many unbelievable features that can make your negotiation easier. Before cell phones were popular (and I realize that dates me), I had a flight phone in my aircraft that I would use to make contacts with potential clients during my travels between engagements. The cost of that flight phone and the call (which at that time was expensive) quickly paid for itself in increased business. Why? Using up-to-date technology to my advantage gave me increased "legitimacy" (see "Legitimacy Power," page 45). Take the time and money to get up-to-date—it could pay big dividends.

Conference calls and/or speakerphones can be used to bring in your expert, or perhaps your negotiating partner (or team). The speakerphone may even be used when you don't have other parties participating. Normally I suggest you ask, "Do you mind if I use my speakerphone?" and either give a reason or don't. Using a speakerphone leaves both hands free to take notes and lets you move about.

Caller ID is also a great tool. It is much easier to say, "Is the number that you called from the best number to reach you or is there a more convenient number?" If you ask the caller for their phone number, they may not want to share it with you. However, if they already know you have their number, they are more likely to give you an alternate number as well. Remember also, when you see that very important negotiation call number on your caller ID, don't answer if you are unprepared to negotiate or if you are in a distracting environment.

In the office, my cordless headset is a great tool. While I'm on the phone I can work on the computer, move from office to office, to retrieve files, and stand up, gesture, or move to a more comfortable chair.

As suggested before, e-mail and text messaging make for additional negotiating tools when telephone and face-to-face negotiating put you at a disadvantage. You should seek to use these written forms of communication when:

- You are very articulate in written communications, and/or the other party is very articulate in verbal skills.
- You are the buyer, and you want to save time.
- You are the seller, and a low-volume buyer tends to take too much time when you contact them face-to-face or by telephone.

Combined with the content of the rest of this book, these eight surefire ways should make you a better telephone negotiator.

10
Team Negotiating

You will never make more money,
than when you are negotiating.
—Roger Dawson

All the information in every chapter of this book applies equally well to team negotiating as it does to individual negotiating. Regardless of how it is conducted, team negotiating presents unique challenges and opportunities. Examining its advantages and disadvantages should help you decide whether to use, or not use, a team in any given negotiation.

You may question how the previous chapter, telephone negotiating, applies. It's simple. It can be effectively accomplished by the use of speakerphones, videoconferencing, or conference calling. Not only can it be accomplished through these media, but in some cases, they may be the method of choice.

You need not think of team negotiation as strictly for a large corporate environment. For instance, suppose your daughter is furnishing her first apartment and she wants to buy a new TV. Another commitment prevents you from going with her. You suggest she take her cell phone and give you a call prior to making a final decision. After she brings you up-to-date on her discussion with the salesperson, you ask her to put on her speaker-phone so that you can join the discussion. Now you have a ready-made team negotiation that allows her to bring in the "expert." If appropriate, you may choose to advise her to check out some other stores before making a decision, unless she gets some other concessions.

If you choose to use a team, the suggestions in this chapter will help you make the most of it.

Advantages

• *Show of strength*. Often increasing the number of negotiators in and of itself provides an advantage be-cause of the apparent show of strength. Carefully ana-lyze each negotiation, however. In some situations, it may appear that you are attempting to compensate for a weak position by large numbers.

• *Moral support*. In addition to the emotional support provided by additional team members, several team members can listen and think while the others talk. This creates less pressure on each team member.

• *Better planning*. My observation of team negotiations indicates that most teams tend to plan more and better than if a single individual is negotiating. Make sure that is the case, however. Obviously, a well-prepared indi-vidual will perform better than an unprepared team.

• *Better internal coordination*. A not-so-obvious advan-tage of team negotiations is that once the negotiations are completed, more people on the negotiating team feel ownership in the decision, simply because they were involved. Internal coordination, or implementing the results of the negotiation, can be greatly enhanced by having more of those responsible for carrying out the results involved in the negotiating process. For this reason, we often see representatives from various departments participating in a particular negotiation because of the significant role their department will play in carrying out or living with the negotiation results.

Example: In a real estate purchase, if remodeling were necessary, it would be wise to have the person responsible for doing the remodeling involved, if not for the entire negotiation, at least for the portion that involves remodeling.

• *Greater expertise.* Adding one or more individuals to a negotiating team simply increases the overall brainpower of the group. "Two heads are better than one" is certainly true here.

Example: In real estate, the team could consist of any number of people—your spouse, an additional partner, a financing expert, an appraiser . . . Their input and insight can only add to the overall expertise of the team.

• *Team members can play different roles:*

   – The Leader
   – The Note-Taker or Recorder
   – The Skeptic or Bad Guy
   – The Good Guy

- The Relationship Builder
- The Body Language Reader
- The Quality Control Expert

Each team member can concentrate specifically on their unique task—before, during, and after the negotiation—to be sure the agreement is comprehensive and then implemented as agreed upon.

• *Less chance of error.* With more people observing the negotiating process, there is considerably less chance of errors. Even a simple error can be costly and significant.

Disadvantages

The advantages above give ample reason for using a team to negotiate. However, there are also disadvantages. You should weigh them against each other before deciding whether to use a team. Obviously, there are times in a corporate or institutional setting when team negotiating is necessary because many people will be involved in the consequences of the outcome. If that is the case, do all you can to minimize the disadvantages by discussing the applicable ones openly with the team.

• *Cost.* It's usually more expensive to have more people involved. Evaluate this carefully to be sure that the magnitude of the negotiation is sufficient to justify the increased expense and/or inconvenience of having more people involved. In the purchase of a home, for instance, increased cost would not be a factor if growing your team means simply bringing more family members into the discussion. However, other factors would be involved (see the following two points below). I would hate to be in the process of final negotiations for a home, with the agent and/or owner present, and have all of my kids yelling, "Daddy, this house is perfect! Buy it, Daddy, buy it. Don't we have to be out of our house by the end of the month?" Enough said. I love my kids, but sometimes . . .

• *Disunity from diverse opinions.* One of the most important disadvantages of team negotiation is that whenever you involve more than one person, you can expect more than one opinion. Certainly, there is more than one successful way to approach any negotiation, but one thing is certain: no approach will work if there is not unity among the team. This is why planning in team negotiation is extremely important. Everyone on the team must know the plan and overall strategy for that negotiation and must be in agreement with that plan. One team member who is out of sync with the group could destroy the effectiveness of the entire team. This is even true in negotiation with your family. The adults in charge will see better outcomes if they present a united front to their children.

• *Confidential information leaks.* In many of my seminars, after discussing team negotiating, a participant will share a horror story where a team member inadvertently leaked confidential information that destroyed the team's otherwise strong position.

Example: The quality control representative who says,

"But their product is the only one that meets our mandatory quality control standards!" . . . A little leak can do a lot of damage!

• *Time*. Most team negotiation takes longer because of the need to plan as a group and to orient each member on the details of the other party and of this specific negotiation. The team negotiations themselves also tend to take longer because more people are likely to add their comments to the discussion, not to mention the time needed to caucus.

SUGGESTIONS FOR TEAM NEGOTIATING

With these advantages and disadvantages in mind, the following suggestions should help your team be more effective.

1. Agree to Show Unity at the Table
Decide ahead of time as a team that there will be no open disagreements at the negotiating table.

2. Caucus to Discuss Differences
Don't hesitate to ask for a break so that your team can caucus to discuss any differences they may have. Differences discussed openly in front of the other party can only create problems for you later in the negotiation.

3. Read Body Language
When a member of your team is speaking, concentrate on the other team's body language. There is no need to

focus on your team member while they are speaking. The skilled negotiator will use this opportunity to pick up valuable body language cues from the other team.

4. Position Your Team for Maximum Impact

If you have the largest team and want to maintain strength in numbers, keep your team seated together. On the other hand, if you have the smaller negotiating team, you may want to disperse throughout the other team, if possible. This may diffuse their show of strength.

If you are negotiating alone, with two or more constituting the other party, position yourself so you can see all members of their team at once, thus enabling you to read all body language cues simultaneously. This position accomplishes one other important consideration: members of the other team cannot signal to each other without you being aware.

PART 4

Perfect Your Game

Going beyond the basics . . .
Strategies that turn a good negotiator
into a great one

11
Strategies and Tactics

Selecting the appropriate strategy depends on three factors:

- Time—the party with the least time pressure wins.
- Risk—often the most powerful strategies carry the greatest risk.
- Needs—all parties' negotiation *and* personal needs play a role.

In previous chapters, I've shared advice that gives you the fundamental skills needed for a successful negotiation. Now that you've learned the basics, let's move to the next level. This chapter will equip you with a toolbox of strategies and tactics to perfect your game. As you begin to understand and master each of the strategies, think of them as tools in your negotiating toolbox, to be used when needed to overcome the complex situations that most negotiations present.

People often ask me the difference between a strategy and a tactic. A strategy is long-term plan, normally used over most of the negotiation. A tactic is a short-term technique, something thrown in here or there in the process of the negotiation. At times, they are difficult to differentiate because it depends on how you use them in a particular negotiation. For that reason, in this book we will not differentiate between them.

Before exploring any of them individually, let's examine four general guidelines that apply to all of them. These guidelines will help you decide when to use (and not to use) each of them:

• *Recognize that timing is extremely important in the use of each strategy and tactic.*

Example: I recall an experience related by a young woman from a very well-known and highly respected Fortune 500 company who came to me at the break of one of my seminars. She shared an experience she had as a new buyer in the purchasing department. She was traveling with a senior buyer from her company to negotiate a new contract with a very important supplier. Less than two minutes into the negotiation, and just after the company had presented their opening offer, the senior buyer folded up his notebook, put it in his briefcase, and was about to leave.

She couldn't believe it! She couldn't believe that this experienced senior buyer was using such a strong tactic as the walkout with this important supplier. "Just then," she said, "the supplier quickly modified his initial offer, and within a very short time, an excellent, long-term contract was concluded."

When they were alone, she immediately asked the senior buyer how often he used the walkout tactic. After a thoughtful pause, he said, "I've never used it before, but the time and the situation were right!" She said, "I'll never forget the importance of timing in the use of strategies."

Some strategies you may rarely use, but, at the right time, in the right situation, the right strategy works wonders.

• *Learn to use many different strategies and tactics.* As I study actual and simulated negotiations, I'm always surprised at the limited number of strategies and tactics used by even some experienced negotiators. They seem to use the same ones repeatedly. They develop habits and settle into a pattern.

On the other hand, the very best negotiators use a great variety of strategies and tactics. Learn them all. Feel comfortable in their use. Practice them, experiment with them until they become a habit and you use them as naturally as you drive a car. Look for ways that you can use different strategies together to be even more effective (such as combining agent of limited authority [page 159] with good guy/bad guy [page 174]).

• *Know how to counter each strategy and tactic.* In order to counter a strategy or tactic's effectiveness, you must first be able to recognize it. Pay particular attention to the counters listed for each of the strategies and tactics discussed throughout this chapter.

• *Never use a strategy or tactic that will destroy the important relationship with the other party.* That is, at least not until you have determined that it is worth the risk. Remember and apply the partnering principles from the introduction when selecting strategies. Strategies and tactics that carry a high risk of destroying relationships include:

- The walkout
- Take it or leave it
- Act and take the consequences
- Lowballing or highballing
- Invoking the competition
- Changing levels

Let's look closely now at thirty effective strategies and tactics and their counters.

1. Surprise

The surprise tactic can take many forms. New information might be supplied, such as the calling of an unexpected witness in a court proceeding. In a team negotiation, a new individual might be introduced to the team, or the personality of a negotiator might change drastically. He or she might become more demanding, for example, or more docile. Its purpose is to destabilize a situation, thereby putting pressure of some type on the other party.

Counter to surprise: Resolve not to be unsettled, shaken, or disturbed, regardless of surprises in the negotiation. Jack Pachuta, a great negotiation trainer and one of my certified licensees, says, "Always anticipate that the other side will use surprise as a tactic. You will come across as cool and collected no matter what happens."

2. Agent of Limited Authority

When the person negotiating doesn't hold the ultimate authority, the strategy is called agent of limited authority. Even though you have the ultimate authority, it may be to your advantage in certain negotiations to have that "authority" limited.

Example: As president of my own corporation, I would appear to be (and in most cases I am) the ultimate authority. However, in many negotiations it may be to my advantage to be an agent of limited authority. Here are the advantages:

- You do not have to make decisions immediately. Actually, you cannot make decisions immediately. The agent of limited authority always has to get final approval from someone else. You have time on your side when you are an agent of limited authority.
- It is the ultimate authority, not the agent of limited authority, who is the "heavy." Therefore, the agent of limited authority is more likely to be able to maintain a congenial and friendly relationship with the other party.
- An agent of limited authority is always able to "save face" when confronted with the need to make concessions. "They finally agreed to what we both wanted."

- As an agent of limited authority, we can always bring in the expert or the ultimate authority, so in essence we can have additional team members.

So, wanting to limit my authority, what can I do? Well, I do have a board of directors. I might suggest to my board to limit my authority on this matter. Therefore, I can truthfully say, "I can't go any further than this without my board's approval. And, quite frankly, I don't think I'd have much luck getting anything more approved." Many people ask their partners, superiors, or even spouses to limit their authority so that they have the advantage of limited authority.

Another example: Recently I was considering a partnership that involved a significant investment on my part. My wife was uncomfortable with the amount of the investment. Reluctantly, I agreed that I would not invest more than the amount with which she felt comfortable. Honestly, my judgment told me that I'd like to invest more, but, hey, I like my wife and I want to keep her! That made me a true agent of limited authority. I can't tell you how much that helped me in that negotiation.

Counters to agent of limited authority:

- Determine the other party's authority level at the beginning of the discussion. You might say, "On transactions like this, are you the decision maker, or do you involve others?" Most often, their ego takes over and they say, "I make the final decisions here!" In this case, you have effectively eliminated their later use of agent of limited authority.

- Arrange to have access to the third party, the ultimate authority, as you are negotiating, so that you can finalize decisions immediately. This is one situation where it may be to your advantage to negotiate at their place of business rather than at yours. Take extreme care not to offend the "agent." Often this counter should not be used for that reason.

- Become an agent of limited authority yourself! If the other side is making only contingent agreements that must be approved by higher authority, you can do the same. What you don't want to have happen is to get to the end of the negotiation, having agreed on all items, only to have the other party say, "Let me go back and see if I can get those last two approved by my boss."

3. A Piece of the Pie (Also called Salami)

Party A concentrates on one small item in the negotiation until they get agreement on that item. In Party B's eyes, the item is too small to cause the negotiation to fail. However, once B grants a small concession, A moves the discussion to the next small item. Each time, B thinks to themselves, "This item is too small to stall the negotiation over." Of course, A's purpose in using this strategy is to ultimately get most of the "pie," which would not be possible if they requested all items at once.

Counter to a piece of the pie: Seek to learn the other party's agenda by asking a question like, "In addition to that, are there any other items we need to discuss before ... [closing the deal ... completing the transaction]?" Alternatively, another question might be, "Other than this request, is there anything else you would like to discuss before we conclude our agreement?" If the other party says no, then you conclude the agreement. If they say, "Yes, there are a few more items," then you say, "Let's list each of them so I can get the big picture." With one or the other of those questions and responses, you can effectively counter this normally effective tactic.

4. Take It or Leave It

Take it or leave it is a risky tactic, but can be very powerful. Its purpose is to force a quick decision because of the possibility of terminating the negotiation over this single item. Although a hard line is sometimes required, this approach is often more effective if presented in these words, "I want you to understand my position. Because of monetary constraints and guidelines given me by my two partners, I have no choice in this matter. My hands are tied. Unfortunately, this is the best I can do." That accomplishes take it or leave it without sounding like a bad guy and, hopefully, maintains a good relationship.

Counter to take it or leave it: Knowing the other party's alternatives is essential, whether this is a true take it or leave it, or a bluff. Carefully weighing *your* alternatives will also be helpful in planning a counter strategy.

5. Forbearance

Forbearance is a delaying or nonaction strategy involving a slow, patient approach to the negotiating process. It works particularly when time is of no essence to you and when your need for agreement in the negotiation is less than the other party's need for agreement. After the opening offer or position is presented (either by you or the other party), you simply do nothing, holding fast to any terms or conditions you have presented and not making any offers of compromise. The purpose of the strategy is to wear down the other party with inaction. In most cases, the other party will begin to make concessions, and the longer you can delay, the more likely they are to do so. This need not be an offensive strategy if, while delaying, you are making soft, understanding comments such as:

- "Carrie, I hope you can understand our position. Your proposal simply doesn't fit within the needs of the master plan for our organization." You may or may not want to explain why it doesn't fit.
- "I can see where your plan would work with some families, but it simply wouldn't work with mine."

In both of these examples, your ability to remain *silent* after your statements makes this strategy particularly effective.

Counters to forbearance:

- Make the time delay costly to the other party. Progressive reduction of an offer, particularly if there is a logical reason to do so, can be very effective.

Example: "John, I must make you aware that our supplier of the main component of Product X [the item

John is seeking to buy] will increase the price by 13 percent in two months. Of course we will have to pass that increase on to you and to our other customers. However, if we could put our agreement together by Friday, I might be able to get management to give you a one-year freeze on our price to you—we would simply stockpile a year's supply of that component part before the price increase. Would you like me to see if I could get that?" The potential for increased savings in this situation may build, and add urgency for the party using forbearance.

• Withdraw an offer or threaten (in a soft, logical way) to do so.

Example: "Tiana, I've just been informed by management that we will be discontinuing this line of products if we are not able to get the part we need from you at the same price as last year. The new line of products was projected to be ready in two years; however, if you can't maintain last year's price to us, our management has made the decision to change over to the new line in three months. We surely have enjoyed doing business with you and hope to continue. What do you think?" Faced with this potential loss of business, this now becomes a top priority for the party that was using forbearance.

• Other counters include using action-oriented tactics, such as the add-on (page 181), act and take the consequences (page 170), and the walkout (page 172).

Always consider the cultural implications in the use of forbearance. For example, forbearance is a much more culturally accepted practice with the Japanese. They are much less likely to make quick decisions.

6. Doomsday

When using the doomsday tactic, the negotiator explains the dire consequences that may result for the other party (or for both parties), if they do not reach an agreement. Its purpose is to force the reluctant party to avoid those unpleasant consequences. It is important to handle this tactfully or the other party may feel unduly threatened. For example, you may want to simply ask, "What would happen if we didn't reach an agreement?" and let them draw their own conclusions.

Example: The purchaser of a piece of property realizes that the owner is facing foreclosure. The purchaser asks, "Miriam, have you ever been through a foreclosure? Are you aware of what happens to the property and the owner?"

Another example: Any labor strike against management is a perfect example of a doomsday for both parties. Tremendous losses on each side are the inevitable consequences if the strike continues. The resolution? A mutually agreeable arbitrator (or arbitration committee) chooses the single most "fair and objective" solution from the one solution submitted by each party.

Counters to doomsday:

• Take the time to carefully weigh options.

- Create an alternative to eliminate the dire consequences.
- Simply ignore the possible dire consequences and take the risk.

7. Funny Money

When was the last time you visited a retail store and bought something for $30.00? You didn't! What did you pay for it? $29.95! Why? Because retailers understand the power of funny money. The number $29.95 sounds like much less than $30.00. So they sell more because they understand funny money, which is simply *presenting things in the light most favorable to you.*

Another way people tend to trick others with funny money is with percentages, which often disguise the magnitude of price differentials. For example, the difference of one-half of one percent may seem insignificant. The fact is that on a thirty-year, $100,000 simple interest note, one-half of one percent represents $12,000.

Example: Years ago, I tried to get my three older children to increase their reading speed. Since I had been a slow reader as a child, I wanted to help them read rapidly. I told them I would put a hundred dollars in each of their savings accounts when they learned to read at least a thousand words per minute. I guaranteed each of them that they would be able to do this in thirty days, if they followed the program for only thirty minutes a day. I thought they would jump at the chance to earn more than three dollars for thirty minutes' work (remember that was long ago and they were young, when three dollars was worth something!). Did they jump at the opportunity? No! Why? You guessed it. It was funny money.

Saving money for some future date does not mean a lot to a kid. I decided to change my approach. The next day I put twenty-one one-dollar bills next to each of their plates at the breakfast table. I told them that they would each receive their speed-reading money a week in advance. I went on to explain, however, that each morning I would ask them if they had worked on the program for thirty minutes the previous day. If they did, they could keep the money. If they didn't, they had to return three dollars to me for the day missed. Not one child ever had to return the money and they all increased their reading speed dramatically. There was no difference in the dollars, only in the way they were perceived. Don't forget funny money in your next negotiation.

Counter to funny money: Reduce all terms to their real value, to real dollars, or to the real cost to you. In other words, use the strategy in reverse—look at the terms of the agreement in the light most favorable to you.

8. Standard Practice

This tactic is sometimes called standard contract, company policy, or industry practice. It is designed to make the other party believe that it is the only acceptable procedure or policy simply because it is the "standard." In other words, it's not negotiable. When used properly, this can be a powerful negotiating tool.

Example: Early in my career, a training director hired me to present a program for his company. As I explained to the training director exactly what I was going to do, he told me I couldn't do it that way. When I asked why, he simply said it was "company policy." I immediately thought, "Who am I, a young and new trainer, to buck this gigantic corporation in regard to their 'company policy'?" The tactic was very effective on me.

Counter to standard practice: Challenge the standard in whatever way seems appropriate. You'll be amazed at what happens when you assume company policy (or industry practice) can be changed—assuming, of course, that it's in *their* best interest as well as in yours. Then it's your job to show them *how*! Make it logical; make it make sense. For example, you are negotiating salary and benefits for yourself at a new job. The people hiring you have told you that both the salary and the benefits package are set by "company policy." Here is where three of the ten power factors in chapter 3 come into play:

- Legitimacy power (page 45): Have you done everything you could do to demonstrate to them that you are the perfect person for this position and that the few extra dollars you are asking for will come back to the company manyfold because of your effectiveness in your new position? If you've done everything you can do there, move to alternative power.

- Alternative power (page 44): What alternatives do you have? Do you have offers from other companies that exceed this offer? Were you considering starting your own business? Changing career paths? Joining your spouse in his or her work? Going back to school? In other words, does the employer know

you have alternatives and how attractive those alternatives are to you? Without alternatives, you lose
much of your power.

- Risk power (page 49): How much risk can you afford
(or are you willing) to take? Are you ready to use
your best alternative as the reason you cannot accept their offer?

These are difficult decisions but if you have explored
your options, you can apply these three negotiating concepts to help you counter this strategy effectively

9. The Nibble

Great negotiators know they can practically always get a
small item thrown in by asking for it *at the time they offer
to close the deal.* Both timing and the size of the concession are critical here.

Example: A few years ago, I was replacing my aircraft.
We had just about concluded a deal. The owner clearly
wanted to sell. His price was a bit high. He had mentioned two minor problems he would fix prior to the
sale. After negotiating the price, I decided to use the
nibble. I mentioned the two items and indicated that I
would pay the negotiated price minus the $500 it would
take me to get the two items fixed back home. (It was a
true nibble—it might have only cost $100–$200 to fix.)
What did he say? "It's a deal!" Compared to the price of
the airplane, $500 wasn't much—but it was $500 extra
in my pocket just for the asking!

Counter to the nibble: Now, here's the important
question for you: What would I have done had he said

no? You guessed it! I would have bought the aircraft anyway and he would have the extra $500 in *his* pocket. Whenever you recognize that someone is using the nibble—remember the deal does not usually hinge on them receiving the nibble. Give it away only when you feel comfortable doing so. Better yet, *reduce* the nibble. If he had said, "That's a good idea, but it will only cost me $100 to get both items fixed, so I'll knock $100 off the price—okay?" I would probably have agreed.

10. Act and Take the Consequences

This tactic involves taking an action that strengthens your position and forces the other party to respond (or else their inaction concedes whatever it is you've done). It is a good tactic to use when negotiating a relatively small item in a large package. Assume that Heather and I have been negotiating a business transaction for some time. When I finally receive Heather's agreement in the mail, I find nine out of ten items of the agreement to be acceptable to me. However, I am not happy with one item. My initial reaction would be to call Heather and discuss the item. Instead, I choose to act and take the consequences. I simply cross out that item, initial it, sign the contract, and return it to Heather.

Now put yourself in Heather's position. What can she do? She has two choices:

- She can call me to negotiate further.
- She can decide that it's not worth risking the whole contract over one small item. Therefore, she initials the change, signs the contract, and we have a deal.

The worst thing that can happen is that Heather decides that deleting that item is unacceptable and we are back in negotiations. Sometimes that will happen, but you will be surprised at how often "act and take the consequences" works.

A young man in one of my seminars had a good story regarding his use of this tactic. He was purchasing a used car, his first one out of high school, and had set $2,250 as his upper limit. The salesperson wouldn't agree to that price. Rather than continue to hassle with the salesperson, he simply wrote a check for $2,250 and gave it to him *unsigned*. The salesperson said he couldn't take it. The young man insisted that he just hold on to it for a few days; his name and address were on the check and the salesperson could contact him if he changed his mind. Two days later, the salesperson was at his door asking him if he wanted to sign the check and buy the car. Obviously, it paid the young man to take the risk. It was better than just walking out. The salesperson had something to think about, and apparently the deal looked better to him later. There is little risk to the act and take the consequences approach.

Counters to act and take the consequences:

- Refuse to accept the changed agreement, and continue negotiations.
- Refuse to accept the changed agreement, and use forbearance (see page 162)—do nothing. The other party will wonder what's happening and will probably contact you. If they do, say: "I'm sorry, we

simply cannot accept that change." Then be silent—do not speak. You now have the advantage.

- Refuse to negotiate at all, if the tactic is used. In other words, you are not negotiating anymore (see the walkout, below) unless they do not use this tactic and retract its previous use.
- Move quickly to your BATNA (see page 82), first letting the other party know that you are moving to your other options, just in case they would like to make a further concession before terminating the negotiation.

11. The Walkout

Just as the word implies, one party walks away from the negotiation (with or without explanation). No doubt about it, walking out is risky. It is also powerful. You have stated clearly that, if the other party does not change something in their position, the negotiation is over. To be effective, the timing must be right. I recommend that this tactic be used only in situations where all else has failed.

Counters to the walkout:

- Make a concession or conditional concession to prevent the walkout.
- Attempt to rearrange some terms of the agreement that may benefit both parties.
- Do nothing. Test the walkout to see if it is a bluff. If you choose this option, you must be prepared to accept the fact that negotiation is over.
- Do nothing, but plan to reenter the negotiation using the techniques in the apparent walkout, below.

- Assume the negotiation is terminated and proceed with your BATNA (best alternative to negotiated agreement).

12. The Apparent Walkout

This differs from the walkout in only one way: the party walking out has a new reason to reenter the negotiation. This tactic is used when you want to bring into play the power of the walkout but eliminate at least a portion of the risk.

Examples of reasons to reenter a negotiation you recently walked out on:

- Your customer wouldn't pay enough for your product. You have just found out that the cost of raw materials (if you purchase them in large quantities) has been reduced, enabling you to make a price reduction (if your client will purchase in large quantities).
- Your final offer on the home you wanted was rejected. The seller was aware that in addition to the price, your other concern was that your children would have to change schools with only three months left in the school year. Now you are returning to the negotiation because you found out that the school will allow your children to complete the school year there, if the parents will provide transportation for the children.
- You rejected the last offer on your vehicle. A week has passed and you haven't had another offer. You call the party that made the last offer and tell them

you would consider splitting the difference. You would actually be willing to take their previous offer, but it is wise to give yourself room to make another concession, and you have nothing to lose with that approach.

Counters to the apparent walkout: Same as for the walkout, above.

13. Good Guy/Bad Guy

You've all seen the good guy/bad guy routine on TV. A tough police officer will be interrogating a suspect to no avail. He leaves and the friendly officer takes over. He's so much more reasonable, the suspect wants to win him over and supplies information the good cop wants. People sometimes ask me, "Can this tactic be used legitimately without faking?" Sure, it can. I find myself using it whenever I go shopping with my wife. One of us wants it . . . one of us doesn't, and we are both being completely honest—simply expressing our feelings.

Example: My ex-wife loved animals and had always wanted a monkey. A local pet store was going out of business and the owner was eager to sell his last animal, a monkey. There was no doubt about it—she wanted that monkey! It was two days before Christmas and I still hadn't purchased her Christmas gift. The price was right, but I was still not convinced we needed a monkey! We already had three birds and three dogs. I was obviously the bad guy . . . but it surely didn't require any acting. The salesperson knew that my wife was the person she had to focus on, and sure enough, we walked out of the store with the monkey—at half the original low, low asking price! That is because no one in their right mind wants a pet monkey!

Example: In a business negotiation, there are many opportunities to use good guy/bad guy, particularly when team negotiating. Say your company is considering adding a new product, if the price and terms are right from the supplier. How easy and natural it would be for the people listed below to play the various rolls indicated:

- VP of sales—wants new product, because it will increase sales (good guy)
- VP of quality control—doubts product quality (bad guy)
- President—feels new product will excite stockholders at meeting next week (good guy)
- CFO—is concerned product can't be profitable, that it has too thin a margin (bad guy)

A team effort here could really make this strategy effective.

Counter to good guy/bad guy: Disarm the team using it by discussing the strategy openly and casually with them. "Boy, it looks like we've got a good guy/bad guy situation going here!" That takes the wind out of their sails.

14. Lowballing or Highballing
The goal of this tactic is to reduce the expectations of the other party by proposing a significantly higher (or lower) offer than the other party is expecting. This is one of the *most* effective and *least* effective tactics: most

effective when the other party does not perceive it as a tactic; least affective when they do perceive it as a tactic. If the other party does not see the high (or low) offer as a tactic, the technique will probably work. If they do, it won't work.

Example: Like the example at the beginning of chapter 4, let's assume you put your house on the market for $450,000. The house has been on the market for three months with no offers. Now I come along and offer $350,000. That may sound ridiculous. However, wait a minute. Suppose I've thoroughly researched the market and show you examples of similar properties that have sold for between $340,000 and $360,000. It is all very clear in black and white. How are you beginning to feel? Aren't you saying to yourself, "Gee, maybe I'm not going to get anywhere near $450,000?" We continue to negotiate and finally agree at $390,000. You would never have settled for $390,000 had my initial offer been $390,000. In short, lowballing (or highballing) is effective when realistically documented with "facts."

Other things being equal, the higher the opening offer, the higher the final agreement; the lower the opening offer, the lower the final agreement. Therefore, make the highest (or lowest) opening offer that you can reasonably justify.

When deciding whether to use this tactic, it's important to consider with whom you are negotiating. Do they expect to haggle a lot? Do they need to get a number of concessions to feel good about the negotiation? If so, this tactic is a particularly effective one. On the other hand, if you are negotiating with someone who likes to put the best (or close to the best) offer on the table up front, and expects you to do the same, I would not recommend lowballing or highballing. People are different, but they are predictably different. Know with whom you are negotiating and make them feel comfortable as far as the process of the negotiation is concerned.

Counters to lowballing or highballing:

- Ask for the reasoning or the rationale behind the offer. "That's an interesting offer . . . how did you arrive at that?" Notice this technique is not confrontational, but simply calm and inquisitive. Now listen carefully. You'll probably hear information that will give you good insight into the other party and their position.
- Simply point out the fact that they are using the tactic to get your attention: "Oh, you're using that old 'highballing' tactic?"
- Be prepared to use your BATNA (see page 82). As discussed in chapter 3, good alternatives give you great power in any negotiation.

15. Feinting (Also Called Reversal)

With this tactic, you appear to go in one direction when you really intend to go in another. It's similar to football maneuvers in that it distracts the opponent from your most important considerations. Many have asked, "How can you use this tactic ethically? Are you not deliberately deceiving people?" Here are two examples of using it legitimately and ethically:

Example: If word were to leak out that a large corporation was considering the purchase of a piece of land in a certain area, the property values would almost certainly go up in that area. The corporation thus uses the feinting tactic. They conceal their real intent. Rather than saying, "We're going to expand here," they say, "We plan to expand somewhere," keeping all options open as they price land in many different locations—eventually, of course, buying the land they intended to purchase all along, but doing so at a reasonable price.

Example: Your spouse and kids have fallen in love with a new SUV. All agree this is the vehicle you want. In approaching the dealership, you would not want them to know your real situation. Therefore, you would gather information from other dealerships and all other options (purchasing online, purchasing a used vehicle, etc.) before approaching the dealership and beginning negotiations.

Feinting is certainly appropriate in this situation. You would certainly *not* want to bring the kids and spouse with you to the dealership.

Counters to feinting:

- Know as much as you can about the party's real needs and interests by doing your homework prior to the negotiation.
- Ask skillfully worded questions (see chapter 1) to bring out their real intent.

16. Cost Breakdowns
A cost breakdown is a buyer's tactic. It enables the buyer to examine each individual item to facilitate cost com-

parisons with the competition, item for item. If there are three parts to the proposal, the buyer may be able to find sources where they can get each at a lower price. This examination strengthens the buyer's position. The request for cost breakdown can present potential problems for the seller. It may not be in the seller's best interest to provide a cost breakdown.

Companies often ask me to provide a proposal for them on multiple training programs—a keynote address, a workshop, and an in-house training program. They want me to give them a total price for all three. After seeing my proposal, they wisely ask, "How does that break down, Jim?" Now, put yourself in my shoes. There is a reason why I can't break the cost down into just three categories (keynote address, workshop, and training program). In order to do a good job on any one of them, I need to spend considerable time researching that company. Now, the cost of that time was spread over the three separate presentations in the proposal. Therefore, if they want a cost breakdown on the three presentations, I would need to add a fourth category—research. That way if they chose just one or two of the presentations, it would include that fourth category, research, which is necessary for any one or all of the presentations.

Have a valid and logical reason why you can't provide a cost breakdown or why a different pricing structure is necessary if you do.

17. Invoking the Competition

We've already established that alternatives give you power in a negotiation. Use that fact. Invoke the competition. In other words, make the other party aware of your alternatives. Remember, if you *have* alternatives and the other party *doesn't know* that fact—it's just as if you don't have those alternatives. It's not who has the power but who is perceived to have the power. Now, what if your alternatives (the competition) are not strong enough? You've got a problem. Develop alternatives that are—or don't use this strategy.

How can you use this strategy and not offend the other party? It's all in the way you approach it. Try saying something like this, "Iracema, I really enjoy doing business with you and I'd like to complete this agreement; but quite frankly, it's just not economically feasible for me. You see, I have this option that is obviously a better deal for me, even though I'd much prefer to work with you. Do you have any ideas?" Leave it at that and see what happens. Put the dilemma on the other party's back.

Counters to invoking the competition:

- Challenge the competition's offer to be sure it is legitimate. Find out as much as you can about the other party's alternatives (i.e., your competition). Are there ways you can get the competition's pricing and other terms of agreement? You might want to say, "From what I know about ABC's pricing and policies, and I know them quite well, that doesn't sound right"—then fall silent. You are hoping that with this probing, yet not confronting, question the other party will share more about the competition's offer.

- Show other differences that make the comparison an invalid one. That is, build your value vs. the competition.
- Add additional options to make your offer more appealing.
- Meet the competition's offer. A last resort. However, the walkout may just be your BATNA (best alternative to negotiated agreement).

18. The Add-On (Also Called Quick Close)

Good negotiators often hold something in reserve to sweeten the deal late in the negotiation. A seller might throw training into the deal at no cost. A buyer might have some value-added item they would provide for the seller who accepts the lower price they are requesting.

Example: The owner of the aircraft I purchased used this tactic beautifully. A few attractive accessories on his airplane were not mentioned in the ad or phone conversations. As we neared the critical point in the negotiation, he offered to throw them in at no additional cost. It sealed the deal as far as I was concerned. Once the aircraft was sold, the items would be of little value to him, but they were of great value to me.

The add-on is the seller's counterpart to the nibble. In the add-on, the seller adds small items in order to close the deal. In the nibble, the buyer attempts to get a few small items thrown into the deal.

Counter to the add-on: Be sure the total package is acceptable. If it's not (even with the add-on), don't accept the offer. If it is acceptable, take the add-on and run.

19. Bracketing

Bracketing is a questioning technique enabling you to determine where the other party stands on a particular item.

Example: You are approaching a manufacturer who could supply you with widgets for your new product, the gizmo. Probing to find a negotiation range, you ask, "I don't imagine it would be possible to manufacture a widget like this for less than $10.00 would it?" Then you watch the facial expressions and body language of the other party to see their reaction. If they seem to agree, then you have established a lower bracket of $10.00. You then say, "I can't imagine it costing more than $12.50." Again, you watch the facial expression and the body language and you get a read on the top of the negotiating range.

Counter to bracketing: Simply be aware that the tactic is being used and act accordingly. Remain aware of your body language in particular, as it can give away more information than you'd like.

20. Changing Levels

When you are not making progress in a negotiation, it sometimes helps to shift to a person at another level. In business, that might be a person at a higher or lower level in the organization. In a family, it may mean talking to the other spouse and sometimes even the kids. It's hard for parents to stand the pressure when all four children are convinced by the salesperson that this time-share vacation package would be the best thing in the world for the whole family.

Changing levels needs to be approached carefully to avoid being offensive. Consider calling on the other party at a time when they might be unavailable, particularly if it might put you in touch with someone who can influence the final decision. In a company situation, you might consider returning to your organization and asking someone at a higher level to contact his or her counterpart at a higher level in the other party's company. It's usually more effective to change to a higher level, but don't discount the possibility of changing to a lower level.

Example: My company was considering the purchase of a new copy machine. It became apparent to me that the salesperson had changed levels downward. He realized that I was the ultimate decision maker, but he also realized the strong influence my office manager had on my decision. He concentrated his sales pitch on her when I wasn't around and convinced her that she really needed this machine. In the end, it became obvious to me that if I wanted to keep my office manager happy, I needed to purchase that copy machine. This was a very effective way to change levels in a downward direction.

Counter to changing levels: Recognize the use, or potential use, of the tactic early in the negotiation, and do what is necessary to prevent it. This might include alerting your superiors to its possible use (with suggestions on what to do if it is used), or saying to the other party, "If there is anything you would like me to bring to the attention of my boss, I'd be happy to do it. He gets upset when someone goes to him directly."

21. Association (Also Called Affiliation)

Very simply, association is intended to associate the party using it with something or someone positive. Advertisers often use this tactic by hiring movie stars, athletes, and other powerful people to endorse their product or service. Why? Well, if the celebrity likes it, you should like it. You can be more like them by having what they have. In essence, they are building their legitimacy power (see page 45) by borrowing the celebrity's.

In the political arena, candidates seek the endorsement of popular politicians—particularly at a level higher than they are—in an effort to be favorably associated with those individuals. Candidates also seek the endorsement of well-established and powerful associations like the American Medical Association, American Cancer Society, American Association of Retired Persons, and many more. Authors and publishers seek to make their books more desirable through endorsements by other leading authors and celebrities. Salespeople seek to make their products more appealing in the same way.

Counter for association: Remember the real benefit or value offered to you, independent of any associations.

22. Active Participation

Active participation is simply asking the other party to put themselves in your position. It is an excellent win-win partnering tactic.

Example: Assume you are negotiating with Fred and he makes a ridiculous proposal to you. There are at least two ways you can react. You can say, "Fred, that's ridiculous. There's no way I can make that work." Not a good response. It escalates the negative.

On the other hand, you can use active participation and say, "That's an interesting proposal, but I'm having difficulty understanding how I can make it work in our organization. Can you help me understand how to make it work, and how to get it accepted by our management?"

This is a good positive response. You are asking Fred to step into your shoes. Perhaps he knows something that you don't, and his explanation will help you see the proposal in a new light. It's more likely, however, that this tactic will enable him to realize that the offer was, in fact, ridiculous. This would make him more willing to modify it.

Counter to active participation: Come up with an explanation that makes the proposition viable for the other party.

23. Feel, Felt, Found
The feel, felt, found strategy can be used whenever the other party has an objection of any kind. As the name implies, there are three sequential steps to this tactic:

1. Begin by agreeing with the individual and saying, "I understand how you feel." People love it! Everyone wants to be understood. It's one of the kindest things you can say, as long as it is sincere and not perceived as a tactic.
2. Next, say, "You know, So-and-so felt exactly the way you feel until they . . ."

3. Then proceed to tell them what So-and-so found, which is, of course, exactly the way you want this person to feel!

That's much better than saying, "Stupid, don't feel that way, feel this way!" Now it is true that you must use a powerful example for the tactic to be effective. Here are a few examples I use:

A meeting planner often says to me, "Jim, I can't afford your fee. It's just beyond my budget." How do I respond?

1. First, I say, "I understand how you *feel*."
2. Next, I say, "So-and-so *felt* exactly that same way." Now it is important here that I select an example of someone with whom the other party can identify, perhaps a familiar meeting planner, or one in the same industry. The strength of the example will determine the effectiveness of the tactic.
3. Then I say, "Until they *found* by their own research that the training program I presented gave them a fifty times return on investment. My fee looked small then. Can I e-mail you the letter they sent me explaining their results?"

Works every time!

Example: A couple considering the purchase of your home likes it but hesitates to buy because it is $50,000 more than they had intended to spend. Understanding the power of feel, felt, found, you say:

1. "I understand how you *feel*."
2. "Quite frankly, we *felt* the same way five years ago when we bought it. We went through an agonizing decision-making period. All I can tell you is that it was the best decision we ever made."
3. "We *found* more satisfaction in this home than we could have ever imagined. Your kids are about the same age as ours were when we moved in. Our family has loved it. What great memories! We wouldn't trade them for anything."

All you need to do now is to be *silent* and let that powerful example sink in. You probably just sold your house!

An important difference exists between the two examples above. The first would be most effective with a person who bases most of their decisions on cold, hard facts. The second would be most effective with a person who bases most of their decisions on feelings and intuitions. Carefully select the type of example that works best with the personality of the other party. People are different. Treat them differently.

Counter to feel, felt, found: Recognize the true value or benefits independent of the association being used in the example.

24. The Flinch

Flinching is a dramatic, negative physical reaction to an offer or proposal. The purpose, of course, is to lower the expectations of the other party. If sincere, and properly used, it can do just that.

Jeanne Robertson, a great humorist and fellow past president of the National Speakers Association, tells an amusing story about her experience with flinching. She is tall and wears a large shoe size. She is accustomed to paying a high price for her shoes. She found a pair on sale for $14.95. She couldn't believe the low price. She asked the salesperson if the price was correct. He said yes. She flinched, not believing the price was that low. He said, "Ma'am [she was in the South], for you, today, the price is only $12.50!"

The flinch, properly used, can be a very effective tactic. Use it anytime your natural reaction conveys a disbelief in what the other party is saying or proposing. If you can't believe their offer is that ridiculously high, let it show in your body language. Don't fake it—if you look like an actor you'll destroy your credibility, but also don't hesitate to let your *real* feelings show.

Counter to the flinch: Recognize it and don't be influenced by it. Some negotiators will *always* flinch, even though they love the offer you presented. Also remember, when the other party flinches, it might be like Jeanne, because the price was too low.

25. External Constraints

This strategy adds some external limit (that you cannot control) to your negotiating range. Its purpose is to force the other party to make concessions because you can't make any concessions due to your externally imposed limit. That limit might be a result of:

- A budget
- A boss
- A business partner
- A committee (whom you are representing)
- A company policy (which you have no control over)
- A spouse (whom you "promised")

Example: My wife uses this tactic effectively. She loves to shop and has become a great negotiator. Before we go shopping, we set certain spending limits. When she sees a particular item that she likes, she is quick to tell the owner how much she likes it. She tells the owner that she knows *the item is worth the asking price,* but she also explains that she is on a budget and can't spend more than a certain amount (and she names an amount). Basically, she's admiring the item and agreeing with the seller as to its value. Then she uses silence. It's up to the other party to make the next move. Often the seller agrees to let the item go for the price she stated as her limit. If not, nothing is lost. The relationship is still strong. There was no haggling over price or what the item was worth. There was, in essence, just two statements of fact made: it is worth the price; and I've only got this much money. Who says effective negotiating has to be confrontational?

Counters to external constraints:

- Change the payment schedule.
- Change the proposal to scale down the cost.

- Challenge the external constraint. They may have fabricated it.
- Use the feel, felt, found tactic (page 185).

26. Reluctant Seller or Buyer

The following scenario depicts a "reluctant seller." Joe puts an ad in the newspaper to sell his boat. Tom comes to look at it. He obviously likes the boat and asks how much Joe wants for it. Joe then says he's decided not to sell the boat because he likes it too much and he's checked prices and can't replace it for anywhere near that much. However, realizing how much Tom wants the boat, Joe says he's curious as to what Tom's top dollar would be. Notice what has happened here. Tom, under these circumstances, is likely to tell Joe the very top dollar he'd pay for the boat.

A young woman who attended one of my seminars shared another great example. She put an ad in the paper to sell her car. On the test drive with the first prospective buyer, she realized how much she liked her car. She explained to the prospective buyer that she had changed her mind and decided not to sell the car. He said, "What was your asking price for the car?"

She gave him a figure.

He said, "I'll take it!"

She said, "No, I really want to keep my car. I really like it."

He raised his offer a significant amount.

She said again, "No, I am really not going to sell."

To her amazement, he increased the offer twice more.

She finally convinced him that she was not going to sell the car.

Now, I'm not suggesting that you act like a reluctant seller or buyer when you really are not. What I am suggesting is that you use timing or other factors to make yourself an honest reluctant seller or buyer. Here is an example of how I did that:

The last move I made was from Green Bay to Phoenix. We had to sell our home in Wisconsin and buy a new one in Arizona. With the move date still in the future, I decided to use time to my advantage. I put my Green Bay home on the market and began looking for homes in Phoenix.

I became both a reluctant seller and buyer. What a great bargaining position! I priced my home slightly above the market. If the right person came along and bought it, I'd be happy, pocket the extra money, and make my move a little earlier.

Similarly, I had my agent looking in Phoenix for just the right home at a bargain price. If the price were right, I'd grab it and make the move slightly ahead of schedule (or even let the new house sit empty for a few months, depending upon the climate, of course—Green Bay winters and Phoenix summers are not the most pleasant times to make a move!).

Counter to the reluctant seller or buyer: Remember this technique is often used as a ploy by the less than honest. Read the reluctant party to determine if that reluctance is sincere or faked. The more you know and can find out about the other party, the better.

27. The Puppy Dog

This strategy gets its name from the scenario of a five-year-old with his parents considering the purchase of a puppy. The store owner is about to close for the weekend. He says, "Why don't you take the little puppy home for the weekend? You can decide Monday morning whether to buy him or not." Is that a sold puppy?

The definition of the strategy is simply allowing the other party to "try" without commitment to "buy" (or "agree"). The purpose is to get the other party emotionally involved—they like it so much they can't say no.

Use this strategy *only* when you know the other party will have a great experience with the "try." It's used all the time at car dealerships, massage chair outlets, in supermarkets with taste testing stations and on TV infomercials—in essence, anywhere the potential buyer will experience positive emotions. This is why so many products and services are offered with a free thirty-day trial or the first three months at half price.

Example: Several years ago, a man was selling me an aircraft. The first thing he said was, "Jim, jump in the pilot seat and let's take it up." What pilot can resist that temptation?

"Have you ever had an aircraft with color radar?" he asked.

"No."

"You'll love this!" He turned it on and explained how safe it would be with my whole *family* aboard.

"Ever have a plane with a Stormscope?"

"No."

"You'll love this!"

Then he got my wife on the flight phone so I could tell her how I was enjoying the airplane! Was I getting excited, or what? Finally, on the approach to landing he turned on the radar altimeter.

"Ever make an instrument approach where you got down to minimums, couldn't see the runway, and had to execute a missed approach?"

"Yes, many times."

"This radar altimeter tells you exactly how high you are when you are making that low instrument approach . . . *with all the kids in the back seats!*"

Did I buy the airplane? Yes.

Did I pay more than I should have for the airplane? I sure did!

However, I learned two important lessons:

- The puppy dog strategy works! So what did I do when I sold the plane years later? You guessed it! I used the puppy dog. And I got a great price for it, too!
- I learned the counter to the puppy dog.

Counter to the puppy dog: Negotiate before you "try."

Imagine what would have happened at the beginning if I had said, "Before we give it a test flight, we've got to talk about the price. I just looked at a similar plane priced $10,000 less, and I've got another one priced $15,000 less that I want to look at before making my final decision *today*."

Would I have been in a much better negotiating position? Unquestionably.

28. The Crunch

The crunch is best described by the statement, "You've got to do better than that!" Its purpose is to force the other side to make a better offer. Those who use it effectively use it even if the offer or proposal is acceptable. The crunch practically always works if the other party is unaware that it's being used.

Counters to the crunch: The next words that come out of your mouth will likely determine the outcome of the negotiation. Here are some options:

- *"Huh?"* Probably the best response. Notice how the pressure shifts to the party using the tactic.
- *Silence.* Same as "Huh?" above.
- *"Okay . . . how much better do I have to do?"* This response implies that you can do better. It is not good here but may be later in the negotiation.
- *"I've looked at this just about every way I can, and I just don't think I can do any better than that."* A nice way of saying no.
- *"I can't do any better than that."* A stronger way of saying no.

29. Humble and Helpless

Humble and helpless is the admission of being in a weak position and trying to use the weakness to your advantage. This strategy works best with people who have a great deal of empathy and who are nurturing by nature. You may want to avoid it with the other more competitive and domineering personality types. The purpose, of course, is to use your weakness and your vulnerability to appeal for mercy from the other party.

Example: You purchased a home a year ago and financed by the owner. You had no problem with the payments until six months ago when you lost your job. Payments began falling behind five months ago and you now owe $5,500 in back payments. The seller has threatened to foreclose and eject you. You have asked for one more meeting with him. Upon meeting you say, "Kellen, I really feel bad about this. You know my situation. You've been very patient with me. I deeply appreciate that. Ashley and the kids do also. You know how I've been trying to find work. I located a job yesterday. It only pays minimum wage, but at least it's something. Ashley is going to get a job also. We sat down last night and figured out a budget. The kids agreed to it. They know there will be no frills—no presents or vacations. However, we can make it work if we can pay you a minimum of $100 per month (plus our regular payment of $1,000) until I get a better-paying job. Beginning next month, Ashley will take an additional $100 out of her paycheck. What do you think? Is there a chance that might work for you?"

You are humble. You are helpless. All you can do is appeal to his mercy.

Counter to humble and helpless: Recognize it as a strategy and evaluate the true position of the other side, not allowing your empathy or sympathy to take total control of the decision-making process. On the other hand, decide whether, and to what extent, you want to use your power to build a long-term relationship (see page 12).

30. Playing Dumb

There are two reasons why playing dumb works so well for many people:

- The tactic itself is disarming. The other party often begins to relax and let their guard down because the other side seems so inept.
- We learn things by playing dumb that we would not otherwise find out because the other party tries harder to explain things to us.

Counter to playing dumb: Recognize the strategy and don't play into it.

Remember it is better to remain silent and appear a fool, than to speak up and remove all doubt.

There you have it, thirty of the most important strategies and tactics in negotiating. Learn them, practice them, internalize them, and, very important, be prepared to counter them. Others will use them against you.

12
Avoiding Common Errors

Truth, like gold, is to be obtained not by its growth,
but by washing away from it all that is not gold.
—Leo Tolstoy

The greater part of this book is devoted to doing things "right" in a negotiation. This final chapter is devoted to avoiding the "wrong" things, the common errors made by even the most experienced negotiators. Ten things done "right" in a negotiation might not overcome one thing done "wrong." Know the common errors. Avoid them. Herein are the true nuggets of treasure that if internalized will make anyone a master of negotiating.

1. Underestimating Your Own Power in a Negotiation

At several advance symposiums held at Harvard Law School, the faculty presented studies that confirm most negotiators tend to underestimate their own power in a negotiation. Why? They are very aware of their own limitations, but not of the other party's. Therefore, there is a strong likelihood that each party will underestimate their own power in a negotiation. When they do, they are less likely to take a risk—further reducing their power in the negotiation.

The skilled negotiator considers this, realizing that

their position is probably considerably stronger than they envision it to be. Making that mental compensation can provide the increased confidence to make the slight edge difference in the negotiation.

2. Jumping to a Conclusion

This is one of the most common errors—making assumptions rather than getting the complete facts. A good example here would be assuming what the other party's needs and desires are, rather than skillfully probing with questions to determine precisely what they are. Herb Cohen says he uses two questions that often help him to avoid jumping to a conclusion. They are, "Huh?" and "Wha . . . ?"

3. Not Understanding the Other Person's Perspective

You are no doubt familiar with pictures or diagrams that project two different images of the same thing, which differ depending on the viewer's perspective. It's amazing the similarity between these examples and a typical negotiation situation. Quite often, there are distinctly different perspectives when looking at exactly the same situation. Skilled negotiators remember this and, rather than working strictly from their own perspective, they probe to learn how the other party is viewing the situation. When you truly understand the other person's perspective, you can better propose a mutually agreeable solution.

4. Focusing on Position, Not Interest

One of the most significant findings to come out of the Harvard Negotiation Project was the understanding that a very common error in negotiation is to focus on the other party's position without probing behind that position to the real interests and needs of the other party.

Example: A common example is that two daughters were arguing over the last orange in the house, which both wanted. Each was concerned only about the other's position—that her sister wanted the orange. A wise father, hearing the dispute, handed one of the daughters a knife and asked her to slice the orange in half, indicating that the other daughter would then select which half she wanted. A brilliant solution? Not really. You see, each of the daughters only got one-half of what she could have had, had they taken the time to look at the interest behind each other's position. One of the daughters wanted the orange for juice; the other needed the peels for baking.

Now, you probably think this is a very simple example and that most experienced negotiators would quickly see through the dilemma, enabling both girls to get what they were seeking. No so! A number of years ago, I developed a business negotiation scenario following this simple juice vs. peel scenario. To date, I have used this simulated negotiation with more than 7,000 top business executives and salespeople all over the world. The teams negotiating over the oranges did not realize (unless they probed for the interest behind the position) that each party had a different use for the oranges. To one, the peel was valuable, to the other, the juice. On the average, less than 20 percent of the teams probed far enough to use both the juice and the peel. As a result, both teams left tens of thousands of dollars on the table.

This example made the point very clearly. All participants learned by experience to *look behind the position, to the real interests and real needs* of the other party.

5. Following the Golden Rule Rather Than the Platinum Rule

Again, people are different. Treat them differently. Treat them the way *they* want to be treated, not the way *you* want to be treated. Remember "Adopt a 'They,' Not 'You,' Orientation," in the introduction (page 9).

6. Entering a Negotiation Without a BATNA

Roger Fisher and William Ury, in the popular book *Getting to Yes*, point out the extreme importance of determining a BATNA, best alternative to negotiated agreement, before entering any negotiation. The only reason to negotiate in the first place is to arrive at a conclusion that is better than what could be achieved without the negotiation. If you take the time to analyze your BATNA, you will know clearly what your "best alternative" is! In the case of a business dispute, your BATNA might be a lawsuit and subsequent trial. In the case of negotiating the cost of a remodeling project, your BATNA might be using another contractor. In the case of a marital dispute, it might be marital counseling. In the case of a labor/management dispute, it might be a strike (by labor) or closing down the operation (by management).

Let's stop to analyze for a minute. The BATNAs listed above are reasonable ones. In fact, they may be your best ones for those four situations. However, brainstorm with me to see if we might create a better BATNA than the one listed above for each negotiation.

- In the case of the business dispute, another BATNA might be taking the dispute to the American Arbitration Association.
- In the case of the cost of a remodeling project, another BATNA might be having your friend help you do it yourself.
- In the case of the marital dispute, another BATNA might be going to a marriage retreat.
- In the case of the labor/management dispute, another BATNA might be submitting the differences to a mutually agreed upon binding arbitrator.

I'm not suggesting that the second suggestions above are better than the first. What I am suggesting is that it is great to have more alternatives to select from so you can arrive at the most powerful one.

One of the major advantages of having the best possible BATNA in every negotiation is that it helps you determine your negotiating philosophy. Whether one is "hard" or "soft," "firm" or "flexible," now becomes largely a consideration of the strength of your BATNA. An extremely strong BATNA allows you to use the more risky tactics of walkout or take it or leave it.

7. Assuming "Their" Problem Is "Their" Problem

Example: I had a client—a construction company—who helped me understand the importance of this common error in negotiating. They had a client who, after several years, developed minor cracks in the concrete driveway supplied by this company. The company was relieved to find that the warranty had expired a month earlier. The customer's problem was their problem. The disgruntled customer, however, found a sympathetic television station that decided to expose what they thought was mishandling of their problem. The extensive negative TV publicity caused the customer's problem to become my client's problem. In any negotiation, think ahead. Don't allow "their" problem to become "your" problem.

8. Getting Hung Up on a Single Negotiated Item

In practically all negotiations, there is more than one item to be negotiated. Whenever this is the case, the skilled negotiator realizes that they need not be hung up on a single negotiated item. Price might be a good example. If price becomes a nonnegotiable item for one party in the negotiation, the other party could concede price negotiations if they got concessions that accomplished the same thing in the areas of interest rates, payment plans, quality, content specifications, and so forth. The successful negotiator looks at the total package and isn't hung up on a single negotiated item.

9. Assuming a Fixed Pie

Many negotiators view each negotiation as a fixed pie; anything I gain, you lose, and vice versa. This normally is not the case because of the many variable factors in the negotiation and the relative value of each of these factors to each party.

Example: I listed a small piece of property for sale

with a very creative real estate agent. Although the listing price was higher, she knew my bottom dollar on the property was $50,000. She came to me one day with an offer for $48,000. She said, "I know your bottom dollar is $50,000, but please examine this $48,000 offer. I'm confident, because of the way it's paid out, it will net you more in after-tax dollars than a $50,000 cash payment would today." I examined the offer, checked with my accountant, and she was right. I accepted the offer. After the closing, I asked her how she worked it out with the buyer. She said, "He wouldn't pay any more than $47,000. However, I knew he had a cash flow problem, so I structured a payment schedule that benefited you from a tax standpoint and helped him with his cash flow. He agreed to increase his offer to $48,000 because of the new payment schedule." That's a great example of a creative real estate agent who did not assume a fixed pie.

10. Not Allowing the Other Side to Save Face

How many times do we see negotiators back themselves into a corner where it is impossible for them to complete a negotiation and save face at the same time? The skilled negotiator understands this and looks for creative ways to help the other party save face, after they have backed themselves into a corner.

Example: When someone says, "This is my final offer," making a big point of it, they have obviously backed themselves into a corner. Good negotiators find additional facts and/or circumstances allowing the other party a logical reason to adjust their "final offer," thus helping them save face.

11. The "One" Solution Syndrome

Many times a negotiator, having done their homework, comes to the table convinced that the solution they have created will solve the problem. Although using advance preparation and creative thinking is always good before a negotiation, don't slip into the "one" solution syndrome. Come to the negotiation table with an open mind, ready to explore all possible solutions.

12. *Offering* to Split the Difference

Notice that "offering" is emphasized. I'm not saying don't split the difference. Simply understand that, when *you* offer to split the difference, it puts *you* in the weaker position.

Example: If I were at $200,000 and you were at $190,000, what would your offer to split the difference at $195,000 do? It would put you in the weaker position. If I were a good negotiator (which I had better be), I might say, "Well, let's see, I'm at $200,000, you're at $195,000 . . ." Whoops! That's not what you meant to imply . . . but you did indicate that you would be *willing* to move to $195,000! Now what might I say? "I'm not able to move from $200,000." [silence] How do you feel now? You are in a difficult position. The longer there is silence, the worse the position.

Now the big question! What should you have done, if you wanted to split the difference? Try to draw that offer out of *the other side.* "Kevin, we are so close. I just want it to be good for both of us. I just want to be fair. Got any ideas? [silence, silence] Now, if I say, "Perhaps we could split the difference," you might say, "Well, if that would be acceptable to you, I can check with my partner and see if it's all right with her. Would that be okay?"

What a skillful job you did! You not only got me to suggest splitting the difference, but you haven't committed yet. I have to commit before you will even check with your partner (agent of limited authority).

13. Getting Too Emotionally Involved

Emotion, and the subsequent loss of reason, is a great cause of error in negotiating. What happens is this. You're in a challenging negotiation and have determined a realistic financial goal. You are so focused on achieving your goal (a financial dollar amount), on "winning" the negotiation, that you lose sight of the big picture, the purpose for which you began negotiating in the first place.

Example: You just located the ideal boat you have been searching for for months. The owner has it listed at $39,950. You figure you should be able to buy it for $35,000. You use all the applicable negotiating techniques that you know. You are still only at $36,500. Here is your thinking at this point. The walkout would have a good chance of succeeding here. You estimate there is a 90 percent chance of buying the boat using a firm and final offer of $35,000. Then you catch yourself before making a big mistake. Ask yourself, "Is it worth a 10 percent chance that I may lose this boat to another buyer for $1,500?" Heck, no. Your ego (emotion) almost caused you to risk losing something you really wanted. Keep your wits about you. Don't let your ego or your emotions bring about something you will later regret.

Conclusion

Successful negotiators have formed the habit of doing those things unsuccessful negotiators dislike doing and will not do.
—Jim Hennig

How can you get the most out of this book?

- Read it from cover to cover, marking points on which you'd like to spend more time. This will give you the big picture of all aspects of negotiating. Note how the chapters fit together, each one forming an integral part of the negotiation mosaic.
- Return to the points you marked, spending as much time as necessary to internalize each concept.
- Prior to your next negotiation return to each chapter, one at a time, and pose questions to yourself, such as:

    - Chapter 1—What information would be helpful to know from the onset? What questions can I effectively use to begin this negotiation?
    - Chapter 3—What factors will affect my power (and the other party's power) in this negotiation?

Where do I stand? How can I use one or more of
these factors to increase my power?

- Take the book with you during certain negotiations
  and, if appropriate during a break, refresh your
  memory on alternatives at an impasse (chapter 7),
  strategies and tactics (chapter 11), handling difficult negotiators (chapter 6), and so on.
- Following the negotiation, review what happened,
  using the book as a guide, chapter by chapter. Determine where mistakes were made (chapter 12),
  what questions could have been asked (chapter 1),
  what you forgot to do when you found yourself in a
  weak position (chapter 5).

Remember that becoming a skilled negotiator is a *process*, not a *single learning event*. An individual can increase
their learning manyfold by actually applying firsthand
the concepts taught in a book or training seminar. Spaced
repetition in learning and applying is the key.

People often ask questions following a seminar or
keynote. Most of these questions have been answered in
this book. However, here are a few important questions
that I chose to save for this concluding section:

Do I want to negotiate at my place (business, home, etc.) or the other party's place?

The answer is to negotiate where you can best control the
environment. This would normally mean your place.
When you control the environment, you gain a significant advantage. How the room is arranged, where tables
and chairs are placed, how the lighting is set, the type and

height of the chairs, all contribute to your ability to create the environment that would best accomplish your goals for the negotiation (see chapter 8, "Body Language").

However, there are circumstances where you might want to consider negotiating on neutral turf or at their location. One reason to negotiate at their place is if you know you are dealing with an agent of limited authority. If the ultimate authority is available on their turf, I would probably want to meet there, thus preventing their later use of that strategy.

In situations where there is no natural starting point, is it better for me to make the opening offer, or encourage the other party to make it?

That is an excellent question. The answer is, "It depends." Here is what it depends upon:

- If you are dealing with someone who you think is very straightforward and sympathetic to your needs, encourage them to make the opening offer. Why? They might just surprise you and offer something better than you expected. You wouldn't want to miss that opportunity. If they did, what would you do? Remember from chapter 4, "Getting and Giving Concessions":

  - Rarely accept the first offer (page 69)
  - Make people work for their concessions (page 70)

- On the other hand, if you are dealing with someone that you think might use lowballing or highballing on you, then you may want to make the first offer. You would then make it as high (or as low) as you could within reason.

Has there been any research done or studies performed that compare the relative effectiveness of women and men in negotiating?

At this point, I am not aware of any research or studies in this area. I have my own opinion based on the thousands of males and females I have observed over the last two decades in both actual and simulated negotiations. I believe there is no substantive difference between their relative effectiveness based on the gender of the negotiators.

Don't people become intimidated when they have to negotiate with you?

I tell them not to be intimidated. I invite them to read my book, listen to my CDs, take my online course, and learn from any other training products or seminars offered. Why would I want someone to know everything that I know? It is simple. My overriding purpose is to help them get what they want as I get what I want. If that is my true goal (and it is!), what is there to be intimidated about? The more we both know about negotiation, the quicker we will arrive at a mutually beneficial solution.

I'm certainly not going to use any negotiation techniques to take unfair advantage of them. I might get by with it a time or two, but they would eventually realize my bad intents and not want to be associated with me anymore. It is true I could keep on finding new victims, but eventually that would run out also.

If you ever have an opportunity to negotiate with me, and I hope you do, read the book first. If you agree with my negotiating philosophy, chances are we'll reach an acceptable agreement quickly.

You've talked a lot about guidelines, strategies, rules, principles, and so forth. Is there ever a time to just operate from the gut—to do what you feel instinctively you should do?

Unquestionably, yes! I look at it this way:

- First, to be a good negotiator you must know and understand the rules of the game—essentially what is discussed and taught in this book.
- Second, you must internalize this information through its use in everyday negotiating. The more you negotiate, and apply these basic principles, the better you become. The more you negotiate, the more these guidelines and principles become second nature to you. They become a habit. And because they have become a habit, they are easy to perform, so you perform them often. You become a good negotiator.
- Third (and this gets to the core of the question), you then begin to get a feeling for the big picture in negotiating, and then your gut will begin to tell you when, and how, you should approach your next negotiation challenge. Ninety-five percent of the time, you will be following the guidelines and principles. However, that remaining 5 percent is very important. That is what separates the good negotiators from the great ones. That is when you begin operating from the gut.

Are some people born good negotiators, or is
negotiation primarily a learned skill?

People are born with certain natural tendencies. Some of us are born with a tendency to be a better negotiator than others. However, I believe this natural tendency plays a relatively small part in our overall negotiating effectiveness. In other words, I believe that if two people were negotiating, one with a natural tendency to be a good negotiator but no training or experience, and the other without that natural tendency but with considerable training and experience, the latter would perform better in virtually every negotiation.

If this observation is correct, and I strongly believe that it is, that is great news for all of us. Regardless of where we are now on the scale of negotiating effectiveness, we are all capable of becoming great negotiators with the proper knowledge and experience. "I'm just a bad negotiator" no longer becomes a valid excuse, unless we *choose* to be a bad negotiator.

What Walter Russell said many years ago is true for us today as negotiators:

> **Mediocrity is self inflicted,**
> **Genius is self bestowed.**

Study and practice the principles and techniques discussed in this book and it will take you a long way toward becoming a "genius" negotiator.

From Australia to Saudi Arabia, from South Africa to Russia, **Jim Hennig, PhD**, is known as a dynamic keynoter, seminar leader, business consultant, and author.

He is a past president of the National Speakers Association in addition to holding its two highest speaking designations: CSP (Certified Speaking Professional) and the coveted CPAE (Speakers Hall of Fame Award).

A frequent speaker and consultant to *Fortune* 500 companies and major national and international associations, Dr. Hennig received his bachelor's degree from the University of Wisconsin and his master's and doctorate from Purdue University, where he also taught for several years. At Wisconsin, he was a member of the University's 1962 Big Ten Championship football team.

Dr. Hennig's business background is diverse. He has been a national sales leader as well as president of four successful corporations in four divergent fields. An accomplished author, he has produced audio/video and interactive

CD-ROM learning systems, as well as books and articles for business and trade publications worldwide. His training materials are available in fifty-two countries and have been translated into twenty-three languages

A heart transplant survivor, Dr. Hennig's energy and enthusiasm are contagious. Hundreds of organizations and thousands of individuals have attested to his ability to inspire, motivate, and educate.

Dr. Hennig lives in Arizona with his beautiful wife, Coreen. They enjoy visits from their ten children and stepchildren and their grandchildren whose number is not revealed because it would need to be updated quarterly.

He can be reached at:

JF Hennig Associates, Inc.
721 N. Lisbon Drive
Chandler, AZ 85226
(480) 961-5050 or (800) 654-5404
Fax: (480) 963-7076
info@jimhennig.com
www.jimhennig.com